More Praise for *The Leadership Gap*

"Drawing from her vast experience coaching senior executives around the world, Lolly paints revealing leadership portraits that expose both darkness and the light in all leaders—and in ourselves. *The Leadership Gap* is fascinating, provocative, entertaining, and useful—a significant new contribution to how we think and act as leaders, and I highly recommend it."
> —Jim Kouzes, coauthor of *The Leadership Challenge* and the Dean's Executive Fellow of Leadership, Leavey School of Business, Santa Clara University

"Thoughtful and practical, analytical and personal, *The Leadership Gap* invites leaders to rethink what it takes to be great, and promises to help bridge the 'leadership gap' that plagues business and society. I urge you to read it."
> —William C. Taylor, cofounder of Fast Company, author of *Simply Brilliant*

"Lolly Daskal reveals exactly what it is that makes great leaders great, along with the gaps that stand between leaders and their greatness. Every leader will benefit by applying the principles contained in this book, along with their people, their customers, and their companies."
> —Emma Seppälä, Yale University Center for Emotional Intelligence, author of *The Happiness Track*

"Today, leaders can only achieve greatness if they are willing to find and fill their competency gaps. In this fast-moving and highly helpful read, Lolly Daskal will show you the seven archetypes of leadership as well as the opportunities and pitfalls each one contains. Read it and soar!"
> —Tim Sanders, author of *Dealstorming* and *Love Is the Killer App: How to Win Business and Influence Friends*

"An Insightful new take on the world from one of my favorite leadership experts. Two Likeable thumbs up for this MUST READ!"
> —Dave Kerpen, author of *The Art of People* and *Likeable Social Media*

"In this deeply insightful book, leadership expert Lolly Daskal outlines a series of eye-opening and game-changing ideas, including why embracing weakness is the first step to achieving greatness. If you want instant insight into your clients, your boss, and even yourself, get this book. It will redefine the way you lead." —Ron Friedman, PhD, author of *The Best Place to Work*

"In these uncertain times, it's more important than ever for leaders to be people who are truthful and who we can trust. This book guides you towards your greatness in the quest to become a better and more effective leader."
> —Lauren Maillian, TV personality, start-up investor, and author of *The Path Redefined*

"This book might just be the next best thing to having your own personal coach."
> —Art Markman, PhD, director of the Program in the Human Dimensions of Organizations at the University of Texas at Austin and author of *Smart Thinking, Smart Change,* and *Brain Briefs*

"*The Leadership Gap* reads like my story—a deep search for 'who I am being while I am leading.' If John Grisham wrote a book on leadership, it would be a compelling page-turner like this one."
> —Chip R. Bell, author of *Kaleidoscope: Delivering Innovative Service that Sparkles*

"I love this book. Each page is chock-full of wisdom and common-sense actionable ideas. Lolly gets to the heart of what keeps us from being great and what we need to do to close the gap to become our best selves."
> —Jesse Lyn Stoner, coauthor of *Full Steam Ahead! Unleash the Power of Vision*

"In *The Leadership Gap*, Lolly Daskal speaks truth to power through her penetrating and practical insights for today's and tomorrow's leaders."

—Bruce Rosenstein, managing editor of *Leader to Leader*, author of *Create Your Future the Peter Drucker Way*

"With expert analysis and soulful compassion, Lolly Daskal provides a fascinating expose on the psychological 'gaps' leaders face in realizing their true potential. I've seen few other books with such thoughtfulness, practicality, and empathy for the human side of becoming a leader."

—Andy Molinsky PhD, author of *Global Dexterity* and *Reach*

"I love love love reading Lolly's leadership insights. She inspires me to be a better man, and her writing gives me effective tools to inspire action in the teams I lead."

—Adam Kreek, Olympic gold medalist and founder of KreekSpeak

"There's no way to read *The Leadership Gap* and walk away unchanged. Lolly Daskal brilliantly distilled her experience working with world leaders into an immediately actionable book filled with wisdom."

—Skip Prichard, CEO of OCLC, author of *The Book of Mistakes* (coming January 2018), and Leadership Insights blogger at www.skipprichard.com

"Great leadership starts with self-knowledge. Lolly Daskal provides a powerful new framework for understanding yourself and rising to become the leader, and person, you want to become."

—Dorie Clark, adjunct professor at Duke University's Fuqua School of Business and author of *Reinventing You* and *Stand Out*

"Lolly Daskal takes us on a unique and insightful journey into the seven archetypes of leadership and shows us what it is that makes some leaders impactful over the long term and others fall miserably short. This book is a powerful tool for growing self-awareness and improving your impact as a leader."

—Dr. Jackie Freiberg, coauthor of *CAUSE! A Business Strategy for Standing Out in a Sea of Sameness*

"*The Leadership Gap* compellingly shows the tension that takes place inside of human beings, because within each of us are two competing sides, but only one leads to greatness. Whether you are a rebel or an explorer, a truth teller or a hero, an inventor, a navigator, or a knight, this book is a valuable resource for anyone who aspires to become a more authentic and complete leader."

—Robert Rosales, founder of Lead Academy, a positive psychology-based leadership development consultancy

"Filled with smart experience and candor, Daskal's book will help any leader get to the next level—including you."

—Damon Brown, author of *The Bite-Sized Entrepreneur: 21 Ways to Ignite Your Passion & Pursue Your Side Hustle*

"Riveting from beginning to end, *The Leadership Gap* pulls back the boardroom curtain to share startling insights from an executive coach who counsels world-class leaders behind the scenes."

—Jane Ransom, international speaker, Success Principles trainer, author of *Self-Intelligence*™

THE
LEADERSHIP GAP

What Gets Between You and Your Greatness

LOLLY DASKAL

DISCARD

Portfolio / Penguin

PORTFOLIO/PENGUIN
An imprint of Penguin Random House LLC
375 Hudson Street
New York, New York 10014

Most Portfolio books are available at a discount when purchased in quantity for sales promotions or corporate use. Special editions, which include personalized covers, excerpts, and corporate imprints, can be created when purchased in large quantities. For more information, please call (212) 572-2232 or e-mail specialmarkets@penguinrandomhouse .com. Your local bookstore can also assist with discounted bulk purchases using the Penguin Random House corporate Business-to-Business program. For assistance in locating a participating retailer, e-mail B2B@penguinrandomhouse.com.

Library of Congress Cataloging-in-Publication Data

Names: Daskal, Lolly, author.
Title: The leadership gap : what gets between you and your greatness / Lolly Daskal.
Description: New York : Portfolio, 2017. | Includes bibliographical
references and index.
Identifiers: LCCN 2016054565 (print) | LCCN 2016055866 (ebook) | ISBN
9781101981351 (hardback) | ISBN 9781101981375 (Ebook)
Subjects: LCSH: Leadership. | Motivation (Psychology) | BISAC: BUSINESS &
ECONOMICS / Leadership. | BUSINESS & ECONOMICS / Motivational.
Classification: LCC HD57.7 .D394 2017 (print) | LCC HD57.7 (ebook) | DDC
658.4/092—dc23
LC record available at https://lccn.loc.gov/2016054565

Printed in the United States of America
1   3   5   7   9   10   8   6   4   2

Book design by Spring Hoteling

To my three beloved children, Michaela, Ariel, and Zoe,
who demonstrate every day what it means to stand in
their greatness

CONTENTS

FOREWORD

When faced with uncertainty, most of us revert to what has always worked for us before. But what happens when that strategy fails? What if there's no precedent for what comes next?

Lolly Daskal's thought-provoking book guides leaders through these uncharted waters, providing them with a rubric for understanding their own character, and tools for skillfully navigating the journey they've undertaken. Drawing on her decades of experience studying human behavior in the context of business, Lolly has created a unique methodology based on seven leadership archetypes—the rebel, the explorer, the truth teller, the hero, the inventor, the navigator, and the knight—in which you will surely see yourself as a leader.

Lolly expertly observes that each of us adopts one or all of these personas at different points in our lives and careers. As an executive coach who has worked with many powerful people, I find that Lolly's insight resonates with me personally. I recognize myself as a natural truth teller!

The archetypes in this book provide an accessible construct for your deeper awareness and ultimately your growth. Understanding which role you embody—when and why—has tremendous value for a leader who seeks to optimize performance. Seeing yourself in each of these archetypes will help you leverage what you do brilliantly well and, by contrast, learn where and why you tend to fail. There are real "leadership gaps" that impede the success of even the most talented executives. By the end of this book, you'll know what yours are, and you will learn how to leverage them.

The need for this guidance is real. In her extensive experience as a coach, Lolly has seen leaders attach themselves to a past version of who they are and insist—even in light of clear evidence to the contrary—that it is still serving them. In my own work through the years, I have counseled endlessly that just because something has worked for a leader in the past doesn't mean it will work in the future. I have warned that the tactics that got leaders to the upper rung of management might be the very things preventing them from rising all the way to the top.

As leaders, we all have gaps in our leadership, and they are not always easy to recognize given that they are so closely entwined with the very talents and skills that propel our success. But humility and vulnerability are the hallmarks of great leadership, and facing the reality of your shadow side is ultimately productive (for a good example, read the story in this book about the executive Lolly coached who hid the fact that he had cheated on his SAT years earlier).

With the kind of coaching guidance that Lolly provides in this book, you are encouraged to admit what you don't know and to rethink your instincts. You'll be motivated to question yourself, which is sometimes difficult for people used to showing strength.

Leaders are encouraged to see themselves not as failures who need to be fixed, but as successful people finding their potential to be even better. In Lolly's formulation, you will succeed by recognizing the heroic archetypes: the rebels, explorers, truth tellers, heroes, inventors, navigators, and knights she describes in such compelling detail here.

Learn how to embrace your archetypes and confront your gaps. I can think of no better way to stand in your own greatness.

—Marshall Goldsmith

INTRODUCTION

Be not afraid of greatness: some are born
great, some achieve greatness, and some have
greatness thrust upon them.

—Shakespeare, *Twelfth Night*

I sat across from one of the most powerful CEOs in America. In the vast window beyond the polished teak conference table, I could see endless blue sky, and in the distance, ships floating in the waterways surrounding Manhattan. But I was not there to enjoy the views from the opulent boardroom. The CEO had called me in distress. His board of directors was in disarray, and as his executive coach I was asked to attend this meeting to provide a solution. Fast.

The problem that concerned the CEO was the dynamic of the directors. Over the past several months, they had become disabled by constant bickering. While there had always been politics among this team of rivals, the tenor had shifted from productive debate to profound dysfunction. The board's inability to agree was negatively affecting the CEO's ability to run the company efficiently.

I sat silently, observing the interactions during the board meeting. Eight accomplished and reputable executives were seated around the table—each a leader in his respective field,* each with years of experience and acumen. In a matter of minutes, I could see the root of the problem.

His name was Richard.

This particular board member was in his own right a highly regarded CEO. Richard had started a technology company that eventually attracted massive government contracts. He was known to be financially savvy; he had made a killing in the market, and it was reported that his net worth soared to the hundreds of millions of dollars when he sold his company.

It was clear that Richard had a keen ability for solving complex strategic problems and making quick, pragmatic decisions—skills he honed over many decades as a trusted CEO. But as he spoke, the resentment he stirred up in the boardroom became palpable. When he was asked a question, his reply was short, clipped, and blunt. In fact, his most frequent response to others was a flat "I know."

Given his success and reputation, I was sure he *did* know. But he appeared to answer before hearing the questions, and he came across as aggressive and arrogant. He created a gap between himself and the board, and his attitude deteriorated the spirit of teamwork among his colleagues.

I quickly recognized that Richard had a problem that high performers rarely confront on their way up, but all

---

* In the interest of clarity and consistency, I am using the singular pronouns "he" and "his" throughout this book. However, it is intended to be gender-neutral. These principles apply to both men and women equally.

inevitably face. It's the one problem that even some of the most successful CEOs I've worked with never see coming and have no idea how to resolve.

The problem is that one day, suddenly, what once worked so well to propel their rise stops working. And the very same traits that had worked *for* them actually start working *against* them. Another stellar career comes to an abrupt end. Another high-flying executive is brought swiftly back down to earth.

This is the moment when leaders confront a critical and very uncomfortable question: What if there's a gap in what I think I know?

Later, when I had the opportunity to speak with Richard privately, I learned that although he had been a CEO for decades, he had never served on a corporate board. His life had become boring in semiretirement and he was itching to feel productive again; so he let it be known that he was willing to lend his expertise and experience to a board. The offers poured in.

Richard was a gregarious man who took great pride in his storied career. He loved talking about his business conquests. He was famous in CEO circles for strategy and implementation, and in our first few conversations, I noticed that he frequently began sentences with "The way I always did it was . . ."

I had seen Richard's style of leadership in action many times before. He embodied perfectly the archetype I call "the navigator": pragmatic, decisive, knowing, and trusted. However, the navigator can develop the leadership gap that surfaces in leaders who become unwilling to admit they don't have all the answers. The navigator then becomes a "fixer": impetuous, arrogant, and egotistical. Richard had become a fixer.

As a CEO, Richard had more than forty years of experience identifying problems and quickly coming up with solutions, so naturally this is what he continued to do. But what escaped Richard was realizing that the skill that made him successful—leading a large organization with decisive direction (that is, telling people what to do)—was no longer serving him. Richard's expertise was what the board needed, but his character was not what they wanted. His leadership gap overshadowed his expertise, and his arrogance was becoming increasingly intolerable. Unfortunately for Richard, he didn't have a clue how his gap was affecting his new position or his board members.

I wanted to help Richard see his leadership gap and to coach him into being the kind of leader others would respect and trust. But although Richard might have sensed something was wrong, he held to his beliefs *because that's what had always worked for him.* How could the skills that had made him successful now be working against him? He refused to accept that his leadership style had become ineffective, or that he was thought to be a know-it-all. He wasn't interested in listening or learning.

This is the mistake that highly driven, overachieving leaders make every day. They have soared to the greatest heights on the basis of what they know. But there comes a time when they must rethink everything and ask themselves: What is the gap between who I am and who I want to be, and do I know what it is I still need to learn?

Richard didn't rethink how his behavior was perceived. Instead, he held to what made him successful in the past, making him, paradoxically, a shadow of his own success. His failure was not due to a lack of skill, experience, or opportunity. His arrogance ruined him.

Richard was asked to leave the board.

Learning to recognize your leadership gap is the factor that determines your greatness as a leader.

Not recognizing it is your downfall.

> The important thing is not to stop questioning. Curiosity has its own reason for existing.
>
> —Albert Einstein

I grew up in a strict Orthodox Jewish community, confined in every way—to a prescribed set of customs, to a particular set of beliefs, to a precise way of thinking, to the perimeters of a neighborhood. Questioning anything we were taught was unacceptably audacious. I persisted in asking, "Why does . . . ?" "How will . . . ?" "What if . . . ?" And the answers, if at all provided, didn't feed my curious mind. I knew if I was going to find answers that would satisfy the curiosity inside me, I would have to fill the gaps in what I knew.

Then, as a teenager, I discovered my own personal font of wisdom: a bookshop on the Upper West Side of Manhattan called Shakespeare & Co.

I became a fixture among the stacks in the shop, and I exchanged ideas and curiosities with the bibliophiles who worked there. Suddenly, my world opened up. I will never forget the day someone introduced me to the work of Viktor Frankl. In *Man's Search for Meaning*, Frankl recounts the suffering he endured in Auschwitz, and exemplifies that a person who finds meaning—significance in his life—could survive anything. That one insight affirmed that my quest for answers was virtuous. I realized that to thrive as an adult, I had to leave my childhood in the past, question what I knew, and rethink how I looked at my life. Frankl taught me that when we can't change a situation we're in, we have to change *ourselves*. He taught me to find meaning in everything I do. He gave me hope for my future.

Over the next few years, I immersed myself in the works of many other great thinkers who challenged my beliefs. Like Carl Jung who taught me that the inner workings of our minds motivate and control behavior. His idea of *archetypes*—personas for our behavioral patterns—continues to influence my work today. To quote Jung:

> Myths and symbols are strikingly similar in cultures around the world and across the centuries . . . in a form of archetypes—symbols that act as organizing forms for behavioral patterns. Each of us is born with the innate tendency to use these archetypes to understand the world.

From Jung, I learned to be reflective and aware of my motivations, to listen to my gut, and to pursue knowledge relentlessly. For years, I featured his words on my Web site, which are still at the core of my own message today:

Your vision will become clear only when you can look into your own heart. Who looks outside, dreams; who looks inside, awakes.

And then there was Joseph Campbell, a masterful storyteller who made famous the claim that nearly all myths share similarities regardless of where they originate. Campbell had a tremendous influence on the way I think, and his work became a key part of my coaching practice. "It is by going down into the abyss that we recover the treasures of life. Where you stumble, there lies your treasure," he wrote,[1] which I understood to mean that even when things don't go the way you thought they would, you can still find your treasure.

But Campbell's most resonant words for me were these: "We must let go of the life we planned, so as to accept the one that is waiting for us."[2] The life I planned was certainly not to be an executive coach and business consultant; but after many years of asking questions, seeking answers, and ardently studying the psychology and the potential of the human mind, I was drawn to this work.

Over decades of advising some of the most prominent chief executives in the world, I developed a coaching style that is rational, a philosophy that is meaningful, and a methodology that is actionable. The essence of my approach is built on the foundation of the seven archetypes of leadership I have seen in action—and the risk to greatness that lurks in the shadows of our leadership gap.

The Rebel, driven by confidence; and the Imposter, plagued by self-doubt.

The Explorer, fueled by intuition; and the Exploiter, master of manipulation.

The Truth Teller, embraces candor; and her twin, the Deceiver, who creates suspicion.

The Hero, embodies courage; and the Bystander, a coward if there ever was one.

The Inventor, brimming with integrity; and the Destroyer, is morally corrupt.

The Navigator, trusts and is trusted; and the Fixer, endlessly arrogant.

The Knight, loyalty is everything; and the Mercenary, who is perpetually self-serving.

Within each of us are two competing sides, a polarity of character, but only one leads to greatness. Regardless of how successful we become, if we want to continue to have a positive impact on the world and make a difference, we must constantly rethink the instincts that drive us.

> At the end of the day, the questions we ask of ourselves determine the type of people that we will become.
>
> —Leo Babauta

My work requires me to spend countless hours in boardrooms, in executive suites, and on corporate jets. I work closely with some of the greatest minds in business and marvel at their talent and expertise. These leaders confide in me, talk through challenges with me, and enumerate hopes and fears to me. I coach every style of leader in every sort of situation—from the explosive crisis behind the scenes to the celebratory press conference. And after years of careful observation, I have identified the leadership gap that separates the best from the rest: *Great leaders have the ability to rethink who they are—they are open to learning, changing, and growing as leaders.*

I believe that leaders at every level and in every position have an intrinsic responsibility to question *who they are being while they are leading.* But it takes a committed leader to embrace the search for truth as a criterion for leadership, and not everyone can achieve this. Very few are willing to embark on an inner journey to discover what propels them.

What prevents so many leaders from achieving the greatness to which they aspire isn't a lack of skill or opportunity. Rather, it's that they rely on what has always worked for them, even when it is no longer working. But it takes a very special individual to own his vulnerability and find his leadership gap. Great leaders want to know, more than ever before, why things begin to go wrong after they have gone right for so long.

Naturally, people look to their leaders for answers, and leaders feel pressured to provide them. But great leaders know that they don't need to have all the answers. What's more important in leadership is asking questions, avoiding assumptions, and pausing to rethink the situation at hand. If you are committed to growing and succeeding as a leader, it is critical that you recognize when there are gaps in who you are and what you know. As a leader, you must get comfortable with the act of questioning yourself. When you stop questioning, you stop learning. And when you stop learning, you stop leading.

This book is for those of you who are looking to create long-lasting success and realize you still have much to learn. It's designed to help you recognize the forces that propel you and understand that what you think you know could be sabotaging you. This book will help you become a better problem solver, a better leader, and a better human. It will help you leverage your leadership gap and find *your* path to greatness.

The essential element of *The Leadership Gap* is a proven system that leaders everywhere can master and apply to their leadership style and life. This book reveals how the naturally occurring patterns in what we think and how we act cultivate our potential. It demonstrates how the greatest leaders persistently ask questions, rethink what they know, and make conscious choices—and it shows what we can learn from them.

Great leaders change the world around them. But I promise you, they start by changing what is within.

I am here as your personal coach, to take this journey with you. In these pages, I speak to you directly in a humble attempt to be of service to you, to help you identify your leadership gap, and to leverage it to become the greatest leader— the best person—you are meant to be. It is *my* life's work to make *your* life's work more meaningful.

—Lolly Daskal

CHAPTER ONE

THE SURPRISING GAP IN OUR LEADERSHIP

*Greatness lies in the gaps between where you
are and where you want to be.*

When chief executives come to me for coaching, they generally want me to help them with any of a vast array of leadership, management, and strategic challenges specific to their situation. I've consulted with executives in almost every industry—technology, shipping, consumer products, pharmaceuticals, finance, and more—and every situation that I encounter is unique.

I work with leaders who are smart, nice, and even power hungry—all at once. Some excel at one quality, yet are weak in another. This is natural—it's the human condition. My job as a coach is to integrate all of an executive's qualities—weak and strong alike—to help him become a more balanced leader.

I have had clients who were masters at solving manufacturing problems, but they could not begin to solve people conflicts. I have worked with great visionaries who could not implement plans to achieve goals. I have had clients who were rapturous public speakers, but they were really bad at listening. Each leader has his own way of being, but the ones who make their mark on the world come to understand that great leadership has many facets, and all must be nurtured. Great leaders learn to expand their talents and develop their deficiencies.

What all talented leaders have in common is that they are good at what they do, and they all want to be great. So, ultimately, my job is to help them identify what stands between them and their greatness—what I call their *leadership gap*.

Many leaders I work with rise to executive roles on the basis of one talent, not realizing that successful leadership requires many. I help them to rethink what they think they know—and pinpoint what they *don't* know—in order to cultivate the skills they never imagined they needed. I know how to spot people with great leadership potential: they are the ones who refuse to be stuck in their ways. They realize that there is a gap between where they are and where they want to be, and they are willing to rethink what they don't know to overcome that gap.

I have seen the techniques I use with my clients change lives, and I want to teach you how to apply these techniques to change your own life.

The chief executives I serve often find themselves in unbelievably challenging circumstances that may appear to have no good solution. As their coach, I help them find the wisdom to make clarity out of complexity, inject meaning into what they do, and give them hope. Some of my clients have responsibility for many thousands of people—each of whom has his or her own needs and problems that demand attention. Regardless of how successful executives become, or how high they fly, we must remember leadership is a privilege.

As Viktor Frankl explained, we never stop hoping for things to be better: "Everything can be taken from a man but one thing: the last of the human freedoms—to choose one's attitude in any given set of circumstances, to choose one's own way."[1] He understood that when we are no longer able to change a situation, we are challenged to change ourselves.

Frankl also understood the wisdom in our gaps. As he once wisely said, "Between stimulus and response there is a space. In that space is our power to choose our response. In our response lie our growth and our freedom."[2]

Without question, my job is to help my clients get to where they want to go in their careers. In my practice, this begins with helping them understand *who* they are—not superficially, but deeply—which means acknowledging the parts of their personality they feel the need to hide or keep secret. These are the parts that have been created and cultivated out of fear, ignorance, shame, or rejection. Together we find the gap that keeps them from becoming who they want to be. Carl Jung calls this gap the *shadow*—"the person you would rather not be."

To make a dynamic shift from where leaders are to where they want to be, I help them *rethink* what they know. My technique for achieving this can be understood through a set of leadership archetypes that were inspired by Carl Jung. My system of archetypes makes it easy to see yourself objectively. Once you have that clarity, you'll have the awareness not only to identify your leadership gaps, but to leverage those gaps from within and to move toward your greatness. You'll be equipped to rethink what you know, what you believe, and what you call truth. The archetypes that are at the heart of this book will enable you to understand yourself and your leadership style in ways you never imagined possible.

It's important to note that I don't believe anyone has one fixed set of characteristics, neatly boxed up in an archetype. A human being is a unique combination of many parts consisting of polarities that create a whole person. I see leadership style as an arc that is in a constant state of movement and change—we shift from one style to another depending on the situation. But at one time or another, in one circumstance or another, we tend to lean repeatedly toward the same archetype persona. While this may be the case, we are in reality an amalgam of all the archetypes.

Take the truth teller archetype, for example. If you're someone who values truth, constantly speaking truth may feel as if it's a force within you. And if you're like Michael, then leading with truth is nonnegotiable.

Michael is an extremely accomplished man who embodies success. And if there's anything that the people who work for Michael know, it's that he has no tolerance for liars. The reason they know this is because Michael talks about it incessantly. He often pontificates about how wrong it is to lie, and how he would never do it. Unbeknownst to Michael, this drives the people around him crazy.

So when Michael discovered one day that many of the people in his organization not only did not admire him for his utmost honesty, but actually wanted to stay away from him, he was shocked to the core. He couldn't understand why people found him difficult simply because his standards were so high. So he sought my advice.

"I'm not sure what I'm supposed to do," he said. "Isn't it a good thing to have high standards? Why don't they respect me?"

I explained to Michael that what he viewed as a high standard—not tolerating liars—was creating a wedge between him and his team, his company, and the other important relationships in his life.

Of course, this was not the feedback Michael wanted to hear and it frustrated him. "I am committed to doing business in a very honest and truthful way. I will not lie," he firmly said, "even if at times my truthfulness costs me in business."

Leadership gaps are invisible and insidious—especially to those who have them. I knew I needed to get Michael to look at himself in a way he never had so that he could rethink not only what he was saying, but what he was doing and why.

I began by asking him questions about his success. He had many great stories, one grander than the next. Then I asked him about his past—what stood out and what propelled his success. Michael's response was focused on his honor, how he avoids lying at all costs, and his belief that because he didn't lie, he prevailed in business. Telling the truth was paramount to Michael.

Once he became more comfortable with me and let down his guard, I had another question for Michael.

"Has there been a time in your life when you lied?" I asked.

At first he just stared at me, his face expressionless. But then his eyes quickly grew more intense, and his body language screamed out to me: *How dare you speak to me in this way?*

But after a long, pregnant pause, Michael answered.

"I always wanted to be a lawyer. As far back as I can remember, I would always tell everyone I would be a lawyer. But I didn't take my education seriously in high school. I thought I could wing it, because everyone said how smart I was. I knew deep inside that if I would just apply myself, I would do well, but I never did. And at the end of high school my report card showed my lack of effort. I knew I was in trouble. My last chance to change things around was to do well on my SAT, so I could get into a great college and law school, and eventually become the lawyer I dreamed of being.

"But I knew I could not learn in just a few months all the information I had ignored during my four years of high school. And then an opportunity came my way that I could not pass up. Someone had stolen the SAT test. I used it to prepare myself with the exact right answers. My high score surprised everyone, including me. I was ashamed and horrified. And when I got called to the principal's office and was asked how I did so well on the test, I lied. Big time."

He cast his eyes away from me, and after another long pause, found my eyes again. "I never told anyone the truth."

We sat in silence for a moment and then Michael regained his composure. "I promised myself, that day in the principal's office, that if I got away with this I would never lie again."

I watched as Michael's pride returned. "It's been more than forty-seven years now. I took that promise to heart—I am an honest man, and I make it my business to always tell the truth."

And there, in front of him, was Michael's leadership gap. We could both see it.

He had been lying to himself for forty-seven years.

Because, you see, what you don't own, owns you.

Michael thought he had come to terms with his lie, but actually it had been wreaking havoc on him for years and he was unable to see it.

Telling the truth became such a strong mantra for Michael that it was getting in the way of his ability to connect with people. But most of all, the way he prioritized truth above all else created gaps between himself and others. This insight was completely counterintuitive to him.

Michael always complained that he was misunderstood. Despite all his accomplishments, he was never satisfied with his life. He feared intimate relationships and he kept friends at arm's length to make sure that they would never discover his secret. He thought his high standards were admirable, but in reality his constant vigilance exhausted him and alienated others. Michael was so afraid of anyone discovering his indiscretion that he avoided getting close to people. Meanwhile, people disliked him and would lie about his positive effect on them, which created a destructive, vicious cycle.

After this moment of clarity, Michael said he felt good for the first time in a long while. He had not realized how he was suppressing his past, or how he carried it with him.

"I can see that you don't judge me," he said.

"I don't," I told him.

After all, I wasn't there to make it right for him, but I wasn't going to let a lie from forty-seven years ago continue to haunt him to this day. I reassured Michael that no one can live up to his standard—*everyone* lies at one time or another.

The next week when Michael and I met for our coaching session, I noticed he looked more at ease with himself.

"Lolly, I don't know why, but I feel so much lighter and more relaxed," he said. "I see things I didn't see before. I am having easier conversations and making connections with people, and I feel more engaged. What did you do?"

I explained to Michael that the reason he felt lighter was because the secrets that create gaps in our lives weigh us down as if we are carrying stones. "Imagine I handed you a grapefruit," I told Michael, "and then asked you to hold it somewhere so that no one would ever see it. The sheer effort of constantly holding the grapefruit would be challenging, but keeping it hidden would be even harder. Your secret was just as burdensome. And over the years it created a wedge—a gap in who you are.

"But when you allow yourself to show someone your grapefruit," I continued, "it relieves you. And it helps you feel lighter, happier, and utterly liberated. By sharing your story with me, you not only released your biggest burden, but now you can see the gap you had created and can leverage that knowledge to achieve greatness."

We are not just what we think. We are what we hide. And we all have something we are ashamed of. The situation may not be as severe as what Michael endured for so many years, but we all have stories we tell ourselves that make us feel vulnerable, angry, and even afraid. These secrets and patterns create our leadership gap.

Once Michael unburdened himself from his lie, he could stop overcompensating for it by emphasizing truth. He could choose to be more human and empathetic—people make mistakes.

Together we worked toward Michael learning to accept himself in all his glorious imperfections. After just one month, Michael was already becoming a much better person, and a greater leader. The change was evident to everyone on his team and in his company. But more than anything, Michael was grateful because now he could be authentic like never before.

Being real is the first step to being great.

As humans we will never be perfect, but we can be the best versions of ourselves. And the way to become the best versions of ourselves is to recognize our leadership gaps, leverage our knowledge in new ways, and stand in our greatness.

It's about learning the two sides of who we are—the side that serves us, and the deceptively identical side that does a disservice to us.

As leaders, each of us must confront our leadership gaps, especially when we're anxious or frustrated or under great stress.

During the course of my many years as an executive coach and adviser, I have found these fundamental truths to be true:

We are all capable of standing in our greatness. Every human being is born with a healthy emotional system. We come into this world without fear, without shame. We don't make judgments about which parts of ourselves are good and which parts are bad. Rather, we dream about doing something bigger than ourselves—we have ideas, thoughts, visions, hopes. Some of us have ideals that are bigger than others', but we all have great visions for ourselves. Until, somewhere along the way, those visions get diluted. Maybe it was the teacher who called you stupid; the parent who said you could do better; the bully who taunted you; the sports coach who called you inadequate. Whatever that message was, you heard it and internalized it. You made the message stick, and because you did, you didn't think you could stand in your greatness.

We internalize our gaps. Leadership gaps are created before we learn what to filter out and what to keep, and we take it all in—including every negative, defeating, pessimistic, cynical, fatalistic, dismissive message. Soon those messages become part of our DNA, whether we know it or don't.

Negative messages create gaps. Once we allow negative

messages to grow, they take on a life of their own. We begin to compensate for dark aspects that we believe are not acceptable to our family, to our friends, and, most important, to us. We learn to hide the things we don't want anyone to see, and we begin to stand in the shadow of ourselves. But we are not alone. Unexpressed fears, horrifying shame, gnawing guilt—these are all obstacles that stand between us and our greatness.

Our secrets create large, deep gaps. When we live in our gaps, we try to hide and deny those parts, or even worse, we try to suppress them. Our gaps are usually made up of the thoughts, emotions, and impulses that we find too painful, embarrassing, or distasteful to accept. So instead of dealing with them, we repress them—seal them away in some part of the unconscious mind, hoping we never have to reveal them. But what we don't understand about our gaps is that the more we try to hide them, the wider they become. Think of a balloon filled with air. When you squeeze one side, the balloon will only grow in size on the other side. The same is true for people.

Consider . . .

- the imposter, who is so insecure he plays havoc with your mind because he has no self-confidence.

- the exploiter, who manipulates every chance he gets just so you will not know how powerless he really feels.

- the deceiver, who is suspicious about everyone because he cannot trust himself to speak the truth.

- the bystander, who is too fearful to be brave, too conservative to take a risk, and too cautious to take a stand.

- the destroyer, who is corrupt and would rather watch great ideas die than not get credit for them.

- the fixer, who is arrogant and a chronic rescuer no one trusts.

- the mercenary, who is self-serving, and puts his own needs before those of the team, the business, or the organization.

The awareness of your leadership gap can be the first step to leveraging your greatness.

When our gaps take control of us, we think we have lost. Our gaps trick us into thinking that we are unworthy, incapable, and unqualified. They fool us into thinking we cannot achieve all the things we want to achieve. But what we don't realize is that we can leverage our weaknesses to get us to where we want to go. Our gaps don't get us lost; they are the principles and qualities that actually help us find our way.

Only when we discover the gaps in our leadership, and confront our shortcomings, can we become truly great leaders.

You must own both sides of the gaps in your leadership. You can't have the good without the bad, you cannot recognize beauty without ugliness, and you cannot know happiness without unhappiness. All of your so-called faults can be your greatest assets. Ironically, understanding your weaknesses is your greatest strength. You have to embrace the gaps in what you know in order to leverage them.

To accomplish this, you have to stop pretending you are something you are not, and you have to own who you really are, even if it makes you extremely uncomfortable. But if you can stand at the edge of your leadership gap long enough, you will see that you are made up of many opposite forces—and that is by design. Once you accept this, you can clear the gaps in your knowledge and make the leap to greatness.

Trust that you can stand in your greatness again. Because your gaps contain the essential characteristics in the script of your life, your job is to learn what the polarities of your gaps are and how to integrate them. Your challenge is to find the value in the parts you think are bad and rethink how they can serve you.

In *The Art of War*, Sun Tzu writes that to know your enemy, you must become your enemy. In the case of your leadership gap, the enemy is the compulsion inside you, which you don't understand or value.

As long as you continue to deny the qualities that make up who you are, your greatness will elude you. But by actively and purposefully reclaiming your gaps, you can leverage them to become the person you are meant to be, live the kind of life you are meant to live, and contribute in the way you are meant to contribute.

The insights you'll discover in the pages that follow will show you how to make your inner life richer, more meaningful, and more actively purposeful. Once you understand and can identify the seven archetypes of leadership, you will be equipped to identify how to recognize the gaps in your own leadership. You can choose to let the gaps become wider, or you can push yourself to leverage them to help you become the great leader you know you can be.

Don't let a gap stand in your way.

CHAPTER TWO

THE REBEL

*The rebel sees something that isn't right in the world,
and then does everything in his power to correct it.*

Juliette Gordon Low founded the Girl Scouts of the USA in 1912. It immediately struck a chord with American girls and its popularity soared. Low's original vision promoted self-reliance and resourcefulness, preparing girls not only for traditional homemaking roles but also to be active citizens *outside* the home. At a time when women were expected to be fully dedicated to their traditional domestic duties, the Girl Scouts encouraged girls to consider professional roles as well—in the sciences, business, and the arts.

By 1918, membership in the Girl Scouts jumped to 34,000. Half a century later, in 1970, it peaked at nearly 4 million. But the seventies were challenging, and by 1980, the Girl Scouts was in a steep decline, losing 1 million members.[1]

The organization had become less relevant and attractive to the new generation of girls, which it needed to survive. The Girl Scouts had lost its direction.

The precipitous drop in membership can be attributed to the fact that the Girl Scouts were increasingly out of touch with the rapid and dramatic social changes of the seventies. Leadership expert Sally Helgesen described the Girl Scouts of the time as "a venerable but relatively staid institution in which girls drawn almost entirely from the white middle class aspired to win homemaker and storytelling badges."[2] And as Jim Collins—author of *Good to Great*—wrote, "The Girl Scouts were in danger of going the way of the Howard Johnson motor restaurants—a classic American icon of a bygone age, increasingly passed by as people's needs and tastes changed."[3]

When an organization seeks to break free of the status quo, the usual practice is to look outward—to hire a new CEO or top executive from outside the company. However, as the threats to the Girl Scouts grew increasingly dire, they promoted one of their own to the top job—a woman named Frances Hesselbein.

Growing up in the small coal-mining town of Johnstown in western Pennsylvania in the 1920s and '30s, all Frances Willard Richards ever wanted to be was a wife and a mother. She married John Hesselbein, the night city editor of the *Johnstown Democrat* newspaper, and gave birth to a son. Frances settled into a life of domestic tranquillity, teaching Sunday school and volunteering at her church.

One day an acquaintance asked her to lead a local Girl Scout troop, but Frances turned her down flat. Frances says,

I carefully explained to her that I was the mother of a little boy and I did not know anything about little girls. Month after month the woman approached me. Finally, she told me a sad story that "in the basement of Second Presbyterian Church are thirty ten-year-old Girl Scouts, and the troop is going to have to disband because they have lost their leader. She has gone to India as a missionary. Isn't it tragic?" After listening to this latest tale of woe, I said, "All right, I will take them for six weeks, and in the meantime you will find them a proper replacement."[4]

Frances recalls the frantic first meeting with her new troop. "It was on a Monday night that I walked into the basement of the Second Presbyterian Church. There were thirty little girls screaming and running around, and for the first and last time, I put up my hand and I said, 'I am your leader.'"

That's when Frances's life changed.

Six years after she agreed to lead her troop, Frances was selected to be the new executive director for the local Girl Scout Council. It had suffered from mismanagement for years and was on the verge of a potential financial disaster after United Way threatened to split ties with it. Frances healed the rift with United Way, installed good management practices, and turned the council around, ensuring that it would be able to serve the needs of Johnstown's girls for years into the future. That success put Frances squarely on the radar of the national organization, and she was later invited to apply for the national executive director position.

Frances recalls telling her husband, John, "I'm sending them a polite letter declining because they're not serious. In sixty-seven years, they have never hired someone to the top position from within the organization. They're not going to start now." But John insisted that Frances at least talk with the search committee. During the course of the interview, Frances was asked to describe the kind of organization she would create if she became executive director.

> I described a quiet revolution. This was a time of great social change—people weren't sure how scouting could be relevant to girls' lives, especially girls from the inner city. We needed to change with the times by questioning everything except the mission of serving girls by helping them reach their highest potential.

On July 4, 1976, the American bicentennial, Frances was named executive director of the Girl Scouts of the USA. She approached the new position with a commitment to rethink all she knew about what it meant to be a Girl Scout. And then she began a remarkable transformation—some would call it a revolution—moving the Girl Scouts organization forward to embrace a much more diverse membership, girls who were hungry for opportunities not previously afforded to them.

Frances made it the mission of the Girl Scouts to reach out to *all* girls—regardless of race or socioeconomic status—and to foster inclusiveness. Frances believed that any girl should be able to see herself as a Girl Scout. One of her first acts was to rethink the old Girl Scout handbook, which was stuck in the fifties. She tossed it out and published four *new* handbooks (each aimed at girls in different age groups) that reflected the diversity of American life. Frances said at the time, "If I'm a Navajo child on a reservation, a newly arrived Vietnamese child, or a young girl in rural Appalachia, I have to be able to open [the Girl Scout handbook] and find myself there."[5] The new handbooks were written to emphasize new opportunities available to girls, particularly in the fields of math, science, and technology.

In addition, Frances rethought the traditional, top-down hierarchy of the Girl Scouts organization and created a new structure of shared leadership—represented by concentric circles that would, in Frances's words, "free people from being stuck in little boxes." According to Sally Helgesen, "This new 'web of inclusion,' as it would be later described, fostered communication across levels and divisions, enabling teams to come together from across the organization, and giving people scope to make their own decisions."[6] The Girl Scout organization was transformed to be more responsive, agile, and able to meet the needs of an increasingly diverse group of girls and volunteers who mirrored the communities from which they came.

Frances Hesselbein's rethinking of the Girl Scouts led to new ideas and innovation that set the organization on a firm foundation for future growth. From 1985 to 2005, total membership in the Girl Scouts grew 38 percent—to 3.8 million,[7] erasing the deficit that Frances inherited when she took the reins of the organization.

Though she might deny it, Frances is a rebel of the first order. She has said, "I am not a rebel—I am just someone who is confident in opening doors. I believe there are no challenges—only opportunities. And to be able to open a door is an opportunity."

Leadership Archetype: The Rebel

> I rebel; therefore we exist.
>
> —Albert Camus

Rebels start revolutions—but not in the way you'd expect. Avoiding revolts and uprisings, rebels are the quiet warriors who embark on quests to achieve remarkable things. They overcome formidable obstacles to save the project, the team, or the company. They ask themselves, **"How can I push the envelope?"**

Rebels are self-assured, confident people who perform extraordinary acts with gentle forms of disruption.

The rebel's strength is driven by his confidence and competence. He has the ability to see when a process, a team, a department, an organization, or an idea can be improved; and he can put all of his efforts and focus into bringing about the necessary change—often quietly, calmly, and behind the scenes, without much fanfare or accolades. Rebels help others discover the confidence within them—enlisting them to their cause. Rebels lead from within.

The Key to the Rebel's Success: Confidence

It is not the mountain we conquer, but ourselves.

—Sir Edmund Hillary

Rebels know they are good at what they do as leaders, and they have the confidence to drive their organizations, and the people within them, far beyond the bounds of the status quo. A rebel isn't necessarily loud or antiauthoritarian. A rebel could have a brilliant, quiet power, like Frances Hesselbein.

Confidence is nothing like braggadocio. It doesn't come from chanting empowering mantras into the mirror, or puffing yourself up in front of others. Confidence comes from skill, knowing that you have the ability to get things done.

The more skill you have, the more talent you have; the more competent you feel, the more competent you know you are; and— ultimately—the more confident you will be.

The equation is simple, but our thinking has not been so simple. I know from observing executives that "playing to your strengths" is insufficient. Of course, you can often get results by doubling down on your natural capabilities. But all successful professionals cultivate a portfolio of traits they can draw from. They do not execute the same play over and over again.

The truth is that the most successful among us—the people who earn their success the hard way—are also the most competent among us.

We have bought in to the idea that confidence equals success; and we are constantly bombarded with quotes, blog posts, columns, and articles that tell us that all we need to succeed is to turn up the knob on our personal self-confidence meter. This is definitely not the case.

Here are a few examples of affirmations people mistakenly believe will give them the confidence they need to succeed:

- Confidence is something you create within yourself by believing in who you are.

- The secret to success is belief.

- If you believe it, it will happen.

Most of these messages give us an incomplete reality. According to business psychology professor Tomas Chamorro-Premuzic, "Biographers are quick to attribute the success of eminent people to their colossal levels of confidence, while downplaying the roles of their talent and hard work, as if it were in anyone's hands or minds to achieve exceptional levels of success merely through sheer self-belief."[8]

We think confidence comes easy but it doesn't.

We think confidence brings us success when it doesn't.

We think confidence is all we need to do well on the job

and in our lives when, in reality, it is confidence combined with competence that makes leaders great.

Entrepreneur and inventor Elon Musk did not find success building businesses like Tesla, SpaceX, and SolarCity only because of his confidence. He found success by merging his confidence with the competence he gained through his university studies in physics and economics. Combined with his deeply held belief in the causes that his companies represent—electric vehicles, space travel, solar power—Musk is quite willing to put his reputation and his money on the line. Musk says, "If something is important enough, even if the odds are against you, you should still do it."

Kiran Mazumdar-Shaw, founder and CEO of Biocon, is widely considered to be the richest woman in India. After her father refused to pay for her medical school education, Kiran decided to become a brewmaster—a job many considered the sole province of men. When she returned to India to become a brewmaster after her training, she quickly discovered that she was not welcome in the industry. So she decided to learn how to produce enzymes, and started a new company—Biocon—in the garage of a house she rented for the business. The company grew, branching out into pharmaceuticals and other products. Today the company that Kiran Mazumdar-Shaw founded has annual revenues of more than $460 billion.

Sir Richard Branson, founder of the Virgin Group—which comprises more than four hundred companies—dropped out of school at the age of sixteen, in great part because dyslexia made learning an incredible challenge for him. However, this did not stop him from achieving a remarkably high level of business success. Branson learned to surround himself with people who are better than he is at specific tasks, and he has leveraged that to his advantage. When you don't have certain skills, you hire the people who do, and the successes gained build confidence.

Achieving the success you want in business and in life takes competence *plus* confidence. I'm certain that Musk, Mazumdar-Shaw, and Branson all went through periods of self-doubt. Branson had businesses go bankrupt; Mazumdar-Shaw was turned away from the brewing industry that she had trained for; Musk has had rockets quite literally go up in flames. But instead of letting failure or the possibility of failure completely derail them, they tried again and again. All three took confident action and learned from their failures. They recalibrated their efforts and eventually claimed success.

Confidence is *believing* you are able.

Competence is *knowing* you are able.

The Rebel's Leadership Gap: Self-Doubt

> Do not allow negative thoughts to enter
> your mind for they are the weeds that
> strangle confidence.
>
> —Bruce Lee

Jeffrey is the CEO of a large aerospace company in Europe. To everyone who knows him, Jeffrey is a rebel—not just today, but *every* day. He is confident and competent, has many responsibilities both in and out of work, and thousands of people rely on him. Sometimes the pressure of his position is particularly difficult for Jeffrey to bear, but he always manages to work through it and keep a firm hand on the tiller of his company. The company is locked in a perennial battle with American aerospace companies, and a recent string of accidents has brought the red-hot spotlight of media attention to Jeffrey's firm.

On the day of our meeting some months ago, Jeffrey looked more serious and worried than I had ever seen him in all the years we had worked together. I could see he desperately needed to talk, and I asked him how he was.

My question triggered an immediate reaction. Jeffrey did not want to talk to me about *how* he was—he had much more on his mind than that. He moved closer, as if he were going to tell me a secret. I immediately became concerned. Was Jeffrey's position with the company in jeopardy? Did something happen since our last coaching session? Was the board of directors about to let him go? Why was my client acting so strangely?

He leaned in to whisper, "I'm afraid they will discover I am an imposter."

Despite his position at the top of the organization, the hard-won successes over the years, the powerful people he interacted with, the deals that were made constantly, and his impressive wealth, Jeffrey was plagued by self-doubt. And he had come face-to-face with his leadership gap.

"I am an imposter, and someday people will figure it out. That frightens me to the core."

"In what way are you an imposter?" I asked him.

"All this success," he told me, "I am not worthy of any of it. All this wealth, I don't deserve it. All the accolades, I am not entitled to them. I sit in a room with very important people—smart people, people who are more capable than I am—and I sometimes wonder to myself, 'What am I doing here? Why am I here? Why are they listening to me?' They are more important than me; they are smarter, better, faster, and wiser than I will ever be; and yet they are listening to me, I am *leading* them. It's only a matter of time before they figure out that I am not worthy of this position."

It wasn't the first time I had heard this same confession in my coaching practice. This is a common leadership gap: According to research, 99 percent of us feel like imposters at least once in our lives.

"Ninety-nine percent of the people in the world who are high achievers, and who are extremely successful, and have made it to the top are just like you," I said. "They feel like imposters. Where do you think the saying 'Fake it 'til you make it' comes from?"

He looked at me and asked, "Seriously?"

I nodded. "Most of the people you work with doubt themselves, and many of the most talented leaders I coach doubt themselves and their abilities on a daily basis. They feel just like you do, but they would never admit it to others because they are deeply afraid of being exposed . . . just like you."

Irrational self-doubt—which takes the form of the imposter syndrome—takes no prisoners; it doesn't care what economic or social background you come from, what field or position you are in, or what talents or abilities you may have. It can be especially hard on high achievers—especially those who are repressing their abilities to be rebels.

Ironically, those who suffer from the imposter syndrome have generally done everything they should do to be successful. They did well at school, earned their degrees, advanced their careers, and often reached the very top of their organizations.

So why would anyone who has achieved great success feel like an imposter? The truth is that people who believe they are imposters don't feel truly competent or that they deserve their success. The imposter makes them believe that they have attained success by getting lucky, simply by being in the right place at the right time. These people may believe they worked very hard for what they have, but they never feel that they have proved themselves, and never see that it was *their competence* that actually got them the success they deserved.

We all know these people.

The medical student who confesses to you over a few beers, "The only reason I got into medical school is because my dad is a well-known doctor and my parents donated a lot of money to the school." Or the female executive who tells you privately, "The only reason I got the job is because they needed to fill the quota for women."

I see men and women who have every reason for being in the top positions of their organizations, but they can't overcome the leadership gap that's keeping them from their greatness. They carry the burden of a very deep, dark secret: the belief that they don't measure up and that they are not as competent as others.

They never believe that their success comes because of who they are and what they are capable of. Fear and doubt are normal, but when you doubt your capabilities, it is impossible to be confident.

If you have failed in the past because you felt like an imposter, you are not alone.

If you have felt like you are a fraud, you are not alone.

The mind will do everything in its power to protect us from our true selves, thinking that this is the right thing to do. The only way we can build the confidence and the competence we need to succeed in life, career, and business is to consider how the mind operates and what our thoughts are really telling us.

The Rebel's Leadership Gap Archetype: The Imposter

It is because we are all imposters that we endure each other.

—Emil Cioran

The imposter archetype is expressed in a variety of different personalities that create gaps in our leadership and keep us from achieving greatness:

Frauds believe that they do not deserve success and that they are pretenders. Frauds are constantly ridden with guilt and feel ashamed about something, and they don't believe they are as smart as everyone thinks they are. They don't think they deserve top positions in their organizations, and they always wonder, "When will the other shoe drop?"

Perfectionists believe any outcome short of perfection is a dismal failure. This belief undermines their confidence and sets them up for failure. There is no such thing as absolute, unchanging perfection—when you have to be the best at everything, you are the best at nothing. Perfectionists don't stop until whatever they are working on is perfect, even if that means spending extra hours, days, or weeks to reach this extraordinarily high standard.

Operators have a list of all the things that need to get done, and don't feel good until everything is working smoothly—which may never happen. Like perfectionists, operators are relentless about getting the work done—perfectly—or they feel worthless. It is impossible for one person in an organization to do all the work alone, so operators set themselves up for failure.

Pleasers think, "Am I good enough? Do I add value to people? If I don't add value, I am worthless." Beneath it all, pleasers think it is impossible for people to like them, so they do everything they can to make people love them. Do more, be more, contribute more—when others take notice, they can think less badly of themselves.

Comparers can't stop reminding themselves that someone is smarter, better, faster, leaner, and wiser than they are. Comparers live in a world of constant envy and have a tendency to be harsh and judgmental. Trying to avoid notice, they create a cocoon of safety by turning the spotlight to others. With such an unhealthy state of mind, the life of a comparer is an exhausting, unending cycle of never measuring up.

Saboteurs have a voice of fear—not just fear of failure, but fear of success. Saboteurs have a way of showing up every time significance knocks and greatness is at the door. They are so frightened of their own greatness that they will do anything in their power to keep playing small, in order to protect themselves from possible failure and shame. This is misguided and incredibly self-destructive when in full bloom.

Leverage the Imposter Within

No one is going to pay much attention to the person who has no confidence in themselves.

—Napoleon Hill

We stand a better chance of developing confidence when we rethink what we think we know, change the way we see ourselves, and cultivate a strong case for our competence, our talent, and our hard work.

Overcoming the imposter gap begins by breaking the chain of self-doubt and understanding how the imposter syndrome suffocates and shackles us. But change is not always easy, especially when the patterns of our lives have existed for so long. Change requires rethinking what we know—the old, outmoded thoughts, patterns, and beliefs that we've carried for so long in our minds—and adopting new, more positive thoughts, patterns, and beliefs.

If you begin slowly, taking on one thought of negative self-talk at a time, I assure you no calamities will occur. You will probably feel that a great burden has been lifted from your shoulders. When you challenge your thoughts, patterns, and beliefs, you will learn how to be less concerned about your doubts. You will become more fearless and unguarded, rather than anxious and filled with worries.

As this happens, you will feel far less like an imposter and more aligned with your competence and your accomplishments. Confidence doesn't come from *saying* the things you *can do*—it comes from *doing* the things *you know you can do.*

Here's how to leverage the imposter within you:

Stop comparing yourself to others. There will always be people who are in front of you and behind you who are doing better than you. Everyone's success story is different, and yours will always be uniquely yours. Instead of always looking at someone else's accomplishments, focus on how far you have come and strive for continual self-improvement in your own leadership development.

Remind yourself there is no such thing as perfect. People who feel like imposters hold the belief that they need to be perfect, but being a perfectionist sets you up for continual frustration because it's unattainable. "Perfect" isn't real, and under no circumstance will you ever be able to master this unachievable idea of perfection. If you are suffering from a lack of self-confidence, and it has led you to feel like an imposter, realize that life and leadership have their successes and failures. Remind yourself that even the most successful people have failed in their lives—many of them numerous times. Make a point to seek excellence—not perfection—and consider a failure to be a learning opportunity and your greatest teacher.

Make a list of your accomplishments. We often overlook how far we have come by taking what we have accomplished for granted. Take measure of your life, and realize that you have overcome many obstacles and that you have enjoyed great accomplishments. Place your wins in plain sight so you are reminded of them regularly. Many people spend more time looking at their failures than focusing on their successes. Remind yourself every day of the things that have gone right for you, and you won't have time to think of what went wrong.

Create an inner circle that supports you. Often you are your own worst enemy and the last one to recognize and acknowledge yourself for your abilities and capabilities. This stems from the idea programmed into us that it is wrong to talk about our achievements and that we should be humble, because otherwise we would be perceived as being full of ourselves. Create an inner circle—your own fan club—that will support you through thick and thin.

When you leverage the imposter within, you can make it your signature for cultivating confidence to be the rebel *with* a cause.

Becoming a Rebel Leader

> Every man who has shown the world the way to beauty, to true culture, has been a rebel, a "universal" without patriotism, without home, who has found his people everywhere.
> —Chaim Potok

Before you can become a rebel leader you must rethink what a rebel is. A rebel leader is supremely confident but can be a gentle warrior, too.

A rebel is the executive assistant who, frustrated by her nonresponsive boss, coordinates a meeting with the company's vice presidents to help her develop a strategy for bringing about change. A rebel is the manager of a team raising money for philanthropic causes; he asks his team members to consider not only raising money, but to be part of the contribution pool. A rebel is the security guard who has advocated for more internal security for years but whose ideas have been ignored by management over and over again, so he sets aside some of his personal time each week to teach and guide employees on the importance of security.

Are you someone who embarks on a quest to achieve remarkable things in quiet ways but with meaningful results? Do you see yourself driven by a deep desire to right wrongs, solve intractable problems, and make a lasting difference in the world around you? Rebels do not seek fanfare or accolades but try to contribute in meaningful ways.

Take these actions to overcome your leadership gap and to achieve your greatness as a rebel leader:

Cultivate self-awareness. Leading with confidence is not about always knowing the answers; it's about knowing what you know and don't know. To be a rebel leader means being honest with yourself about your competence and your personal strengths and weaknesses; neither underestimate nor overestimate your capabilities. Be aware of the leadership gap of self-doubt because the worst enemy of confidence will always be your insecurities.

Assess your skills. As a leader in pursuit of greatness, it's critical to objectively identify your skills and competencies, and constantly work to improve what you can to become what you believe you can be.

Part with being perfect. Striving for perfection will not get you to your greatness. Perfect people aren't real, and real people aren't perfect. Becoming a great leader doesn't mean perfect. It only means you're able to live with your imperfections.

Stop comparing yourself to others. When you compare yourself to others, and are being critical about yourself, this is never constructive. When you compare yourself to others, it is a battle you will never win. The greatness you seek is in understanding that you will never be anyone else, and no one else will ever be you.

Learn to be adaptable. In today's business environment, adaptability is an important element of your leadership skill set. On any given day you might be collaborating with your team, and the next hour you might be presenting to the board, or dealing with a disgruntled customer or client. Whatever the situation, it's key to be adaptable, to be flexible, and to have the confidence to think fast on your feet. Great leaders go with the change as the change is happening.

Stay strong when the rest go weak. Great leaders stay strong and confident when things become most challenging. Not only does *confidence* allow you to make the tough decisions that people expect from a *strong leader,* but it reassures and realigns those around you who sometimes have doubt.

Be driven by a cause. At the heart of every rebel is the belief that you can contribute in a meaningful way and make a difference in the lives of those around you. Rebels look for worthy causes and opportunities to make a positive impact.

GREAT REBEL LEADERS

Rosa Parks famously took a seat on a bus, in confident defiance of institutionalized racial discrimination.

Elon Musk takes risks that other CEOs wouldn't even consider, and as a result he inspires the world to rethink everything, from the cars we drive, to how we power our homes, to the future of space travel.

Gloria Steinem has the confidence to question social norms and challenge long-established expectations of women. Her confidence has motivated millions of women to express themselves and challenge the status quo.

Every organization and every company needs rebels with the confidence and competence to lead teams to places they may not go on their own. Becoming a great rebel leader begins with closing the leadership gap within you and overcoming self-doubt. Do not allow your inner beliefs about yourself to keep you from achieving what you know you can. Embrace the rebel within; know you are deserving and capable. Be responsible to yourself and accountable to others. Lead as a rebel by encouraging each member of your team to discover his own inner rebel and bring it to bear on his life and work.

You'll find your greatness there—just beyond your self-doubt. Go and claim it.

Recognizing Yourself in the Rebel Archetype

The rebel is confident about a cause and is willing to oppose the status quo in order to save the day, team, company, and organization. The rebel is willing to stand up for something bigger than himself.

Are you a rebel? Ask yourself these questions:

- In what ways do you resist the status quo?

- What are your key objectives as a leader?

- What gets in the way of your confidence?

- In what ways do you assert your independence?

- What do you believe in so strongly that you are willing to fight for it?

- When do you feel like an imposter?

- Does self-doubt plague you, and if so, under what circumstances?

CHAPTER THREE

THE EXPLORER

*The explorer knows when to rely on his analytical mind,
and when to rely on his intuitive mind.*

The morning of April 24, 2013, was the same as any other in Dhaka, the capital of Bangladesh. The high temperature was predicted to be 91 degrees for the day. The sky was hazy, and the streets were alive with the rattle and hum of people rushing to their jobs in local businesses and factories. The Rana Plaza building complex in Dhaka was one of these factories, producing a steady stream of inexpensive garments for a variety of different companies around the world, including Benetton, Bonmarché, Walmart, and others.[1]

At 8:45 a.m., without warning, the power went out and five generators started up, shaking the building.[2] Moments later, there was a loud explosion and the eight-story Rana Plaza building collapsed, leaving the first floor intact, but crushing everything—and everyone—in between. According to Manzur Ahsan, a fireman who was at the scene of the tragedy, the building was "stacked like slices of bread."[3] Inside, more than 3,000 people were trapped in the rubble—some alive, some dead, and many more critically injured.

All told, 1,134 workers in Rana Plaza died as a result of the injuries they sustained in the building collapse.

An ocean of clothing is produced in near-slavery conditions around the world by many millions of people (85 percent of whom are women), often in steaming-hot, overcrowded, and unsafe factories and homes. Industry estimates indicate that somewhere between 20 and 60 percent of total garment production worldwide is accomplished by homeworkers. According to journalist Lucy Siegle, these homeworkers—often helped by their children—are "hunched over, stitching and embroidering the contents of the global wardrobe   in slums where a whole family can live in a single room. They live hand to mouth, presided over by middlemen, tyrannical go-betweens who hand over some of the lowest wages in the garment industry."[4]

This situation raises a moral question: Should thousands of people in developing countries have to live in poverty and give their lives every year to allow us to buy cheap clothing? For Safia Minney, founder and CEO of the fashion label and retailer People Tree, the answer is an unequivocal no.

Safia grew up in the UK with a love of design, textiles, and documentary photography. Her father (who died when Safia was seven years old) was Mauritian and her mother

Swiss. Her grandmother was trained in embroidery design at a young age, and Safia was inspired by her intricate, hand-stitched work. A book of her father's—*The Family of Man*—sparked a love for documentary photography. "As a child," says Safia, "I loved the way it portrays people from the developing worlds as genuinely happy and resilient, not down-trodden."[5]

As a teenager, Safia worked at a local market, and she made regular visits to charity shops to pick through the clothing, looking for fashion gems. "At seventeen, in my first job in London," says Safia, "I'd spend my tiny salary on clothing that other people didn't want—I really developed my eye for fabric and print then."[6]

Already an explorer as a teenager, Safia Minney founded People Tree in Japan in 1991, with the express mission of turning the global garment industry business model upside down. She saw how fast fashion was exploiting and manipulating the world's most impoverished, and she was inspired to do something about it. Disturbed by the knowledge of what was causing harm to so many poor, Safia built the first clothing company in the world to guarantee fair-trade standards and environmental production practice throughout its supply chain. Instead of exploiting workers, People Tree committed to doing business in a way that protects human rights and supports environmental innovation in the clothing-manufacturing process. Safia says, "We are deeply committed to empowering the poor, protecting the environment, and changing the kind of world we live in."

For Safia Minney, rethinking the business of fast fashion inspired a new paradigm that is more sustainable, more profitable, and much more fair to the workers who produce it: *slow* fashion. According to the company,

> People Tree is a different kind of fashion business. We give customers an alternative to fast fashion. The fast fashion industry is fueled by insatiable demand for cheap clothing and accessories. Fast fashion has a devastating impact, from sweatshops and child labor to pollution and global warming. Slow Fashion means standing up against exploitation, family separation, slum cities and pollution—all the things that make fast fashion so successful.[7]

Leadership Archetype: The Explorer

Man cannot discover new oceans unless he has the courage to lose sight of the shore.
—André Gide

Safia Minney is a consummate explorer, driven by intuition to create new paradigms. Explorers are the pathfinders, pioneers, and seekers who drive organizations, communities, and the human race forward. They are dissatisfied with the way things are, and are restless to find new approaches, new solutions, and new ventures. Explorers use their intuition to test the boundaries and limits of what is known. They reject the status quo and doing things just because they've always been done that way. They ask, **"What can I discover?"**

As an explorer, you are obsessed with rethinking the way things are commonly done. You question conventional wisdom, and are motivated to reassess processes and establish new business models in search of innovation and improvement. The explorer rejects old, dysfunctional ways and is eager to adopt breakthrough ideas. If you are an explorer, you are guided by intuition. You are constantly thinking and rethinking what you know, and you instinctively—almost automatically—know what to do, what comes next, and where things are going.

The Key to the Explorer's Success: Intuition

Knowledge has three degrees—opinion, science, and illumination. The means of instrument of the first is sense, of the second dialectic, of the third intuition. This last is absolute knowledge founded in the identity of the mind knowing with the object known.

—Plotinus

Explorers are *intuitive*—they listen to their inner voice and their gut, and use the knowledge gained to make decisions. Instead of relying only on their rational thought processes, they balance their thinking with a strong infusion of intuition. Explorers are extremely important for the advancement of humanity, our organizations, our leadership teams, and our communities. Explorers constantly look for ways to make a difference—both small and large—and they want to change people's lives.

When someone knows something intuitively, he feels and knows it with certainty. It is much more than a hunch; it is a visceral knowledge that, if given attention and credence, can become useful in thinking, producing new ideas and innovations, and making decisions.

Intuition means different things to different people.

Some call it a *gut response.*

Others call it a *burst of genius.*

Some call it a *breakthrough.*

The language of intuition is short and concise, and it usually shoots through your mind in the form of a command.

"I want this."

"It feels right."

"I can't do it."

"It feels wrong."

Take a close look at these statements—do you notice anything in particular about them? According to author Mary Goulet, we recognize them because they are intuitive; they are statements that are concise and simple—usually just five words or less.[8] The moment you add on the word *because,* your mind has shifted from intuition to becoming logical and analytical. It happens in a split second—so quickly that you don't even notice the transition.

Intuition doesn't make us confused; it does not make us doubt. It feels clear and concise.

Intuition doesn't give us reasons. It won't tell you why, where, or how.

A decision made using our intuition usually has no agenda and no emotional attachment to any particular outcome. It just *knows*. It just feels *right*.

Intuition is knowledge based on experience, stored deeply within the brain, and available quickly and on demand. It is a way of knowing that still defies rational explanation, although researchers continue to look for clues on how it operates.

It's clear that these snap judgments—these glimpses of intuitive power—are often extremely accurate. When combined with our analytical mind, the decisions that result can change the world.

Here's how to cultivate intuition:

Answers are the rewards of wisdom. Learning never ends. The more you learn, the more you know; the more wisdom you accumulate, the more the answers will seem obvious to you.

You must fill the arsenal. The nature of the explorer is to accumulate an arsenal of proficiencies, so that when you bump up against a problem, your solutions come quickly, swiftly, and decisively.

Trust your inner sense. Intuition, or your gut instinct, is your omnipresent sixth sense—and just as important as the standard five. Intuition informs the process of self-communication, moving information from the subconscious mind to the conscious mind.

Know your proficiencies. Assess what you are capable of doing and what you still need to learn to get the job done. Have the insight to know when to take action and when not to.

Take decisive action. Explorers trust themselves implicitly. They rely on their intuition to take action. When your intuition is strong, follow it.

The Explorer's Leadership Gap: Manipulation

> There are those whose primary ability is to spin wheels of manipulation. It is their second skin and without these spinning wheels, they simply do not know how to function.
>
> —C. JoyBell C.

As a consultant, I'm often asked to work on business strategies with organizations and companies. These strategies are created in workshops where participants are given the assignment to develop a compelling business case for change. They are also tasked to create a detailed implementation road map, efficiently and effectively manage the change process within the organization, and measure progress against relevant metrics while building alignment across their organizations.

These workshops usually bring together the most important people in the organization—including the leadership team, and sometimes operations, finance, human resources, and information technology—all working together during an intense week of meetings.

These strategy sessions are demanding, and as a consultant, I am hired to ask the hard questions to get the right answers. The process to develop strategies is different for every organization I work with, and I have learned to be patient with the process. In the end, it is always successful.

One workshop in particular—conducted for a large pharma multinational with a name almost anyone in the world would recognize—was especially difficult.

The meetings were held off-site, at a large conference facility in the foothills of the Rocky Mountains. The air was clear and the location quiet, and we made a point of turning off our smartphones and laptops so we could put our full energy and attention into solving the issues before us.

On the first day of the workshop, the conversations were intense, and the interactions were harsh. There was little alignment within the group. No one could agree on the best way to move forward. The company's CEO—Oskar—just wanted to talk numbers. And he was adamant.

As the workshop facilitator, I was responsible for creating the elements of the strategic plan with the team. There were more tough conversations throughout the second day, and as it was coming to a close, I reviewed our progress (or the lack thereof) and it became very clear where this group needed to go.

Oskar was a dysfunctional CEO. He was certain he knew better than others, and he used manipulation to get what he wanted. He ignored the need to make his people feel important, and he failed to give them the vision and guidelines they needed to build an effective strategy. I knew that there was a tremendous leadership gap and that if we continued down this road we would not succeed. I had to convince him to dramatically change his approach.

Given Oskar's penchant for the hard realities of analytics, data, and numbers, he was not going to be a pushover for any soft suggestion I might have. Oskar had risen through the company ranks—starting as a summer intern while he was in college and working his way up from there. He was always sure of what he wanted and how he wanted it done, and this morning was no different.

"Let's get this done," he said. "We just need to implement what we have done before—it worked last year."

"We can't," I said.

"Why not?" asked Oskar.

"Because most of your people worked hard—no, they worked *really* hard," I replied. "But the only definitive direction they got from you last year was to make more money. That will not work this year. Last year you got lucky, but this year you won't be so fortunate. People want more direction from you.

"Things are changing," I continued. "The markets are more volatile, customers are more finicky, and globalization will drive this organization to be faster. You have to take this all into account—you cannot tell your people to just make more money and expect them to understand exactly what they are supposed to do."

"It will work," he said. "It always works—the numbers add up."

"It's not always about the numbers," I told him. "There are many more variables at work in your organization—not least of all the needs of your people."

But the CEO remained firm in his thinking, and I continued to push him to rethink his position. I pointed out the gap in his leadership, and I didn't back down.

"Maybe you don't know how much better it can be," I ventured. "If you keep doing what you do, but with more direction, your people could perform even better this year. Don't you want to see that?"

Oskar wasn't about to back down either. "The numbers work," he said.

"Creating a successful organization isn't always about repeating what you did last year, and it's not always about using your rational thinking," I explained. "Not everything is present in the analytics. You have to take *everything* into account—your people, your processes, your practices. You have to give your people something they can grab on to. What you're doing won't work."

Before Oskar could counter once more, I made a suggestion. "Bring in the rest of the team," I said, "but this time don't manipulate the conversation, and don't exploit your leadership position, and let's see what they say. In fact, encourage them to explore some options."

Oskar halfheartedly agreed with my suggestion, which was just enough of an opening for me to prove my point to him.

Soon all the participants arrived and took their places in the room. It was our last day—and it had been an intense few days; everyone was exhausted. I stood in front of the room and asked, "What does everyone *think* about the strategy we developed during this week's meetings?"

In unison, everyone nodded their heads, agreeing that it was a good one.

I then asked, "If you could stop *thinking* about your strategy, and instead explore how it *feels*, what would you change?"

Everyone was quiet, furtively looking at their leader, Oskar, for direction. They were so used to Oskar's approach to leadership—or the lack of it—that they were afraid to speak up.

I told them that we needed to rethink the strategy, to make sure that it not only made sense but that it felt good. It needed to be something they could take back into the company, to their teams, to the people they worked with, and deliver on their targets.

I asked again, "How does this strategy *feel*?"

I looked directly at Oskar, and I said, "Let's start with you. How does it feel?"

"It doesn't feel right," he said solemnly, with deep conviction—letting everyone in the room know that these were his true feelings.

This opened up the floodgates for the other employees. As I went around the room, the answers from the leadership team ranged from "It has no energy," to "It has no heart," to "It has no engagement," and "It's all very rational, but maybe it won't be possible to make happen."

As each person spoke, I nodded my head in agreement. I then walked over to the huge whiteboards filled with information and formulas and strategies from our sessions that week.

And with one big swoop, I erased it all.

When I turned around, I could see on their faces that they were in a state of shock, and even panic.

But then I said, "Now let's work together and explore what your intuition tells you is right."

And for the next six and a half hours, with few breaks, we worked feverishly on what *felt* right. We talked about people, engagement, and strategy, but this time with heart.

In the end, we looked at the new work we had done together, and I again asked the CEO and his team, "How does it *feel?*"

"Great!" everyone shouted in unison.

This group of very clever and smart men and women instantly understood that success sometimes requires intuition. More important, sometimes rational thought can lead you down the wrong path. I invited the team to trust their gut in this case. In the end, the strategies they developed proved to be the right ones for the company.

The Explorer's Leadership Gap Archetype: The Exploiter

> The most successful exploiters are the ones who make others feel that he or she has their best interests at heart.
>
> —Randall Collins

The leadership gap for the explorer archetype is the tendency to use intuition to manipulate others in order to gain control. When leaders don't allow their employees to think for themselves, when they micromanage or become controlling, they are leading with manipulation.

They become exploiters.

Exploiters cannot reap the benefits of even the most talented team because, like Oskar, they tell them what to think, what to do, and how to do it. If someone doesn't feel he can speak up to his boss, showcase his talent, or is unable to be seen as a contributor to the organization, that person will feel manipulated and exploited.

Unfortunately, exploiters are not an anomaly—in many

organizations you will hear leaders telling their people, "Do it my way or you are out!"

Manipulative, exploitive leaders are easy to recognize:

They set themselves up as the expert. Rather than being a real expert, the exploiter uses information to confuse others. He'll rattle off facts or impart esoteric information that team members wouldn't understand. The exploiter seeks to overwhelm others with his knowledge, and he succeeds when the team feels a sense of incompetence.

They withhold information. Information is power, and the exploiter wants it consolidated with him. He withholds information in order to make others feel less secure, less competent, and less confident. This is a play for control, and if confronted, the exploiter will claim that others don't need or shouldn't have certain information.

They are mercurial. Though the exploiter may come across most of the time as pleasant and sometimes even kind, if he is crossed or disappointed, the wrath will be unleashed. Exploiters don't show their cards, and it is never clear which personality will respond—the nice side or the one to fear. Exploiters enjoy the spectacle of others tiptoeing around them, fearful and submissive.

They make threats. Because the exploiter leads with manipulation, he persuades others by using subtle force or outright threats. He may yell, criticize, or threaten people to get the action he wants. Exploiters commonly use terms such as, "If you do not do this, I will___," or "I won't___until you____." This is a manipulation tactic used to exercise control.

Avoid becoming an exploiter: concentrate on what *brings* value while being careful not to destroy *what* you value. Remain cognizant of *who* you are being as you are leading.

Leverage the Exploiter Within

> Leaders trust their guts. "Intuition" is one of those good words that have gotten a bad rap. For some reason, intuition has become a "soft" notion. Garbage! Intuition is the new physics. It's an Einsteinian, seven-sense, practical way to make tough decisions.
>
> —Tom Peters

Closing the leadership gap between an explorer and an exploiter begins with recognizing the fine line between intuition and manipulation. Whereas intuition makes things better for others, manipulation is always about making things better for you.

The leadership style prevalent in the twentieth century advocated for controlling outcomes, exercising power, and manipulating consequences. But the time has come to rethink that approach. Manipulation creates gaps within us and between us and those around us. In the highly competitive, fast-paced, modern business world, teams must collaborate effectively to gain an edge.

In his book *The Creative Executive,* management consultant Granville N. Toogood describes how *Wall Street Journal* reporter Thomas Petzinger Jr. sees the future of business:

> Petzinger believes successful companies in the next economy will operate more like organisms naturally developing and growing in cooperation with one another, rather than man-invented hierarchical machines marching to strict work rules—stifling novelty and using employees more as drones and less as creative and intelligent beings in their own right.[9]

The future that Petzinger predicted is *now.* Leaders must reject the old, hierarchical ways of leadership—the "my way or the highway" approach—for their teams to thrive and be successful. Exploitive leaders destroy cooperation with headstrong manipulation. In today's environment, every person in every organization must tap into every advantage available— the future of business depends on it. Here's how:

Don't take advantage of people's weaknesses. Instead of preying on the weak, look for ways to praise people. The last thing you want to do is take advantage of the person who does the most for you. Anyone who takes advantage of someone else's weakness doesn't deserve the use of his strengths.

Don't use people's weaknesses against them. Everyone

has a weakness, a gap within him. The weakness is usually insecurity, or an uncontrollable emotion or need. Most of the time, people are ashamed of their weaknesses and try to keep them secret. When you use people's weaknesses against them, it's because they remind you of your own weaknesses. So stop putting other people down when deep inside you feel inadequate. Anything that annoys you is here to teach you a lesson. Anything that angers you is here to teach you compassion— not only for others, but for yourself.

Don't make others give up something in order to serve your own self-interest. An exploiter always has an agenda, but what he doesn't know is that, for most people, it is pretty easy to spot. And most people will not tolerate it. If you wonder why you don't have a group of people around you who respect you, trust you, and are loyal to you, maybe your exploitation has gotten the best of you.

Mean what you say and say what you mean. Remember that the exploiter will often say what you want to hear, but that doesn't mean he means what he says. Exploiters get satisfaction in being able to have power over others, but this power never lasts. If you want the people around you to respect and trust you, start by being mindful of what you say. When you make a promise, keep your commitment. When you say you will do something, do it.

When you take ownership of the parts of yourself that want to manipulate and exploit others, you take the first step in leveraging the gaps in your leadership.

Becoming the Explorer Leader

We are all inventors, each sailing out on a
voyage of discovery, guided each by a private
chart, of which there is no duplicate. The
world is all gates, all opportunities.
                            —Ralph Waldo Emerson

The explorer who overcomes his leadership gap and becomes
a great leader has learned when to rely on his analytical mind
and when to rely on his intuitive mind. In any given situation, both instincts are powerful, and both offer valuable direction. But intuition is one of the strongest attributes to have
within your leadership tool kit. The intuitive leader is a valuable asset for his organization. Insight and knowledge have
their place, but great leaders are comfortable with their intuition and lead with it.

The idea of intuition, although ancient and mysterious to
many, has always been a source of critical decision-making
since the beginning of time. Intuition continues to fascinate
researchers as it makes headway in the sector of leadership
and management. Arguments in favor of the importance of
intuition in thinking are widespread in contemporary research.

Many consider intuition to be a sixth sense. Simply put,
intuition is the process of how our subconscious mind communicates to our conscious mind. Although the communica-

tion comes from within, we don't necessarily trust it. According to psychologist Gary A. Klein, "Intuition is an important source of power for all of us. Nevertheless, we have trouble observing ourselves in this way, and we definitely have trouble explaining the basis of our judgments when someone else asks us to defend them."[10]

Intuition is regularly explored and exhibited by highly successful leaders all around the world, yet it is hardly a topic of conversation in organizations today. Leaders rarely discuss their intuitive hunches or their gut feelings—perhaps because it would seem to their peers as an unscientific or illogical approach to management. Using intuition could appear to be weak, and no leader wants to appear weak to others. But with my training, leaders and organizations have come to appreciate the value of intuition, and they work to improve their intuitive-thinking skills. Intuition fosters greater success and higher profits, better decision-making, and more sustainable levels of innovation and service.

The process by which most leaders and managers have been trained to think is analytical, logical, and filled with reason. But sometimes analytics and logic are insufficient, and leaders must rethink what they know. The explorer leader uses his intuition when a problem becomes too complex, or when the left side of the brain (the logical side) does not have enough information to fuel a solution. Ideally, the right side (the visual and creative side) and the left side of the brain work in harmony to solve a problem.

In the words of management thought leader Peter Drucker:

> When approaching a business problem, don't try to come up with the answers. . . . Focus on what the problems are. . . . If you get the wrong answer to the right question, you usually have a chance to fix it. . . . But if you get the right answer to the wrong question, you're sunk. . . . And business does altogether too much of that.[11]

Stephen Harper, a professor of management at the University of North Carolina, Wilmington, puts it this way:

> Because of their experience in making judgment calls, intuitive executives have the courage to sail into uncharted waters. Most managers are reluctant to make a decision—even though one must be made—because they do not have enough data or prior precedent. The intuitive executive, however, will not hesitate; he will tap his knowledge for direction and action.[12]

To follow our intuition or ignore it is always a purposeful choice. It takes trust and tenacity to be an explorer. Here are other defining characteristics of the explorer:

The master of innovation. The explorer looks for things to change, improve, or infuse with new vision. He craves the adventure of finding new things in old places. The explorer is willing to make dangerous, difficult, or unique journeys for the main purpose of disrupting things.

The gift of vision. The explorer has a unique ability to envision new realities and a need to feed his ideas to the world. He has the discipline for intense, careful, and thorough research; and he creates by first reading, studying, and talking to people.

The power of self-assurance. The explorer believes he can make a difference and is driven to. He is bolstered when others condemn his plans as delusional, crazy, impossible, or stupid. The explorer has the self-assurance to push himself to new, exciting places—and his company, team, or organization to new lands.

The ability of persuasion. The explorer has extreme passion for his ideas and learns how to sell his vision to others. He works to perfect his presentation skills—whether formal or informal. The explorer is a master at the skill of building support.

The capacity of decisiveness. Every leader is sometimes required to make decisions quickly. An explorer leader has an edge: powerful intuition. He isn't afraid to make commitments swiftly without running the numbers first. He is comfortable relying on what limited data he can gather, trusting his gut to make a decision. In other words, the explorer leads with intuition.

The balance of rationality. Rational thinking can become a hurdle when it paralyzes your analysis, blocks intuition, focuses too much on perfection, highlights fears, and prevents new learning. The explorer doesn't force his mind into boxes; he allows it to be free in order to reveal what he already knows.

The quintessence of preparedness. The explorer maintains game-day fitness—emotionally, physically, and mentally. He is equipped to withstand those who would knock him down and question his vision—especially those who resist following intuition. The explorer understands that his greatness won't come from doing what everyone else is doing; it will come from doing what he knows is right and pushing past boundaries.

GREAT EXPLORER LEADERS

Jeff Bezos is gifted with powerful insight about the potential of the Internet and the future of retailing. Now he is making headway into the final frontier—space.

Sara Blakely not only created a product, she created an opportunity—a solution to a problem women didn't even know they had. Now she's a self-made billionaire.

Neil deGrasse Tyson is an American astrophysicist and the director of the Hayden Planetarium. As a true explorer of space and black holes, he has intuitively changed the way science has been made accessible to us.

Intuition is a prized business and leadership skill that only a few gifted leaders know how to tap into effortlessly. However, we all have intuition; it's just a matter of recognizing it, developing it, learning to use it, and getting comfortable depending on it. In a world where uncertainty is a constant, having something utterly reliable is an incredible asset. Leaders can solve even the largest, most intractable problems when they learn to leverage their intuition and apply it to their decision-making.

The enlightened executive, the intuitive leader, will routinely rely on his intuition when it comes to solving complex problems—when logic is not the right way to go. There are leaders who will use their intuition, and leaders who will use only their logic and analytical mind.

The best kind of leader—the explorer—uses both.

The language of the explorer's intuition is a concise and persistent command from within:

Intuition is your inner guide that leaves reason to the side. Some say intuition is the language of the soul; others think it's the heart of the person; others believe it is the unspoken words of your truth. However you define it or experience it, there is no denying that intuition is an integral part of leadership and our lives.

Everyone knows what it is like to struggle for something of value. It is our drive that keeps us yearning for something better for ourselves and for the world. We want the unfairness of our society and the injustices of the world—like the exploitation of sweatshop workers in Bangladesh—to be addressed. It takes all of us—all the explorers in our businesses—to use our intuition, knowing what is right, what is just, and what can create a better future for humanity.

We need explorers in the world—those who know how to make us rethink what we think we know.

To disable poverty, disease, and ignorance, we need the explorer.

To dismantle bureaucracy and ineffective organizational designs, we need the explorer.

To dismiss arrogance, egotism, and pomposity, we need the explorer.

We must trust our instincts and recruit, encourage, and promote leaders who have intuitive insight. This insight is becoming mandatory in organizations when it comes to decision-making, creativity, and innovation. Our customers demand intuitive insight from us; our clients are cognizant of it; and our consumers will pay a premium for it.

If you seek greatness, you need the heart and intuitive mind of the explorer.

Recognizing Yourself in the Explorer Archetype

The explorer is intuitive and has a compelling desire to discover who people are, including himself, while using his intuition in making decisions and taking actions.

Are you an explorer? Ask yourself these questions:

- In what ways do you explore as a leader?

- In what ways are you intuitive?

- Do you trust your intuition? Why or why not?

- How do you tap into your intuition?

- In what ways do you use manipulation to get what you want?

- Do you evaluate decisions and situations based on your gut feelings, or after a thorough analysis—or both? How do these different approaches affect your outcomes?

CHAPTER FOUR

THE TRUTH TELLER

The truth teller is driven by a sincere desire to help and will speak out courageously when his honesty serves others, even at the risk of offending people.

To many, football has replaced baseball as America's favorite game, but in reality, it is much more than that. Football—specifically, the National Football League (NFL)—is a business, a very *big* business. According to estimates, revenues for the league's teams total more than $10 billion a year, and 25 of those teams are each worth at least $1 billion or more. In a recent year, more than 17 million fans attended NFL games—paying on average $84 a ticket—while 202 million more fans watched NFL games on television.[1] As commissioner of the NFL, Roger Goodell makes $44 million a year—an amount that eclipses the heads of all other sports leagues and most corporate CEOs.[2]

Understandably, the NFL is extremely sensitive to anything—or anyone—that might threaten the lucrative cash cow that has enriched the teams' owners and the NFL's leadership.

On September 24, 2002, Mike Webster—a former center for the Pittsburgh Steelers and the Kansas City Chiefs football teams, whose professional career spanned seventeen years—died at the relatively young age of fifty. Considered by many to be the best center in football history, Mike was a four-time Super Bowl champion, a nine-time Pro Bowl participant, a seven-time All-Pro, and a member of the NFL Pro Football Hall of Fame. He also endured an estimated 25,000 violent collisions with other players during the long course of his career. It was determined that—at the time of his death— Mike Webster had suffered from a variety of physical and mental ailments, including bone and muscle pain, amnesia, dementia, and depression. He was addicted to prescription painkillers and Ritalin, out of money, homeless, and divorced. He lived for some time in a pickup truck before he died[3]— surviving on Pringles potato chips and Little Debbie pecan rolls.[4]

Immediately after Mike Webster died, his body was taken to the Allegheny County Coroner's Office in Pittsburgh for a routine autopsy to determine the cause of death. There, forensic pathologist Bennet Omalu was assigned to perform the autopsy. Dr. Omalu—born in 1968—immigrated to the United States from Nigeria in 1994 to complete a fellowship in epidemiology at the University of Washington in Seattle.

According to a report in the *Washington Post,* "Watching coverage of Webster's death (the cause was not released), Omalu was shocked that the people who talked about him on television mocked his intelligence. Omalu wondered if perhaps Webster suffered from *dementia pugilistica*, or punch-drunk syndrome"[5]—an affliction often suffered by boxers, whose sport inevitably exposes them to repeated blows to the head. The condition causes memory loss, dementia, dizzy spells, speech problems, tremors, explosive behavior, and more.

However, when Dr. Omalu removed Mike Webster's brain for examination, he was surprised to find that—at least on the surface—it appeared to be completely normal, without the contusions that would be evident in the case of dementia pugilistica. This puzzled Omalu—a neuropathologist by training—who was convinced that there must be some sort of mechanism at work that caused the football great's severe mental decline. So he decided to take a closer look at the football player's brain. At his own expense, Omalu had special brain tissue slides prepared, and he viewed them through a microscope. What he saw through the microscope's lens surprised him: the telltale red flecks of abnormal tau protein that are the result of repeated blows to the brain. Omalu recalls, "I had to make sure the slides were Mike Webster's slides. I looked again. I saw changes that shouldn't be in a fifty-year-old man's brain, and also changes that shouldn't be in a brain that looked normal."[6]

Concerned about the potential implications for the health of other professional football players, in July 2005, Omalu published a paper about his findings in the medical journal

Neurosurgery. In this article, Omalu dubbed the condition he discovered *chronic traumatic encephalopathy,* or CTE. He was convinced that the NFL would receive his findings with open arms and use them to "fix the problem." But Dr. Bennet Omalu was wrong.

Instead, the NFL began a vigorous campaign to cover up the findings—refuting any connection between football and CTE, and doing everything in its power to discredit Dr. Omalu. Soon after Omalu's paper was published, three doctors on the NFL payroll—Ira Casson, Elliot Pellman, and David Viano—demanded that *Neurosurgery* retract Omalu's paper. In their letter to the editor, the NFL-paid doctors said, "These statements are based on a complete misunderstanding of the relevant medical literature. . . . Omalu et al.'s description of chronic traumatic encephalopathy is completely wrong."[7] The journal declined to retract the paper.

In the meantime, Dr. Omalu was assigned another autopsy of a high-profile football player—this time former Pittsburgh Steelers guard Terry Long, who committed suicide at the age of forty five after a long history of symptoms almost identical to those of Mike Webster. He, too, suffered from memory loss, depression, and psychotic behavior—and he was bankrupt and living alone. When Dr. Omalu examined samples of Terry Long's brain, he found the same telltale red flecks of abnormal tau proteins. It was CTE. Dr. Omalu published another paper in *Neurosurgery*—this one based on his findings in the Terry Long case.

By this time, the issue of CTE and professional football players was gaining attention in the press, and Dr. Omalu was at the center of the storm. When reporters asked the NFL about Dr. Omalu's findings, the responses were swift—and negative. "Preposterous." "It's not appropriate science." "Purely speculative." A friend warned Dr. Omalu that by speaking the truth about his discoveries, he was putting himself in danger. "You are challenging one of the most powerful organizations in the world," Dr. Omalu was told. "There may be other things going on that you're not aware of. Be careful!"[8] Dr. Omalu's own father called him from Nigeria, fearful of what could happen to his son. "Stop doing this work, Bennet. I have heard not nice things about the NFL; they are very powerful, and some of them not nice!"

Yet Dr. Bennet Omalu continued in his quest to tell the truth—regardless of the pressure for him to stop. He examined the brains of two other high-profile football players—former Philadelphia Eagles safety Andre Waters and former Pittsburgh Steelers lineman Justin Strzelczyk. The results were the same: CTE.

In 2007, as pressure in the media continued to grow, NFL commissioner Roger Goodell convened a concussion summit. Invited to the meeting were doctors and trainers from every football team, along with a group of scientists. Notably absent from that group of scientists was Dr. Bennet Omalu, who had by then become public enemy number one in the eyes of the NFL. Neurosurgeon Julian Bailes—a colleague of Omalu's—commented on the situation, "They were trying to blackball him, lock him out, marginalize him. He was the whistleblower."[9]

According to Peter Landesman, director of the film *Con-*

cussion, which told the story of Dr. Omalu's quest to bring the truth about CTE to the public's attention, the NFL and its allies threatened Omalu and his family in a variety of ways—trying to silence him. "Bennet was followed," says Landesman. "He was pursued very often. He would come down to his parking lot and find all four tires of his car punctured a number of times, happened a number of times. They were terrified they'd be deported. He was essentially chased and hounded out of Pittsburgh."[10]

Ultimately, Dr. Omalu was forced to resign his position with the Allegheny County Coroner's Office and find employment elsewhere. He eventually accepted a job as chief medical examiner for San Joaquin County in the rural Central Valley of California.

Dr. Omalu's career was ruined, his professional reputation tarnished, and his personal life torn apart—all by an NFL organization that was more concerned about its bottom line than it was about the veteran football players whose lives had been destroyed by CTE. In Omalu's words: "I was naive. There are times I wish I never looked at Mike Webster's brain. It has dragged me into worldly affairs I do not want to be associated with. Human meanness, wickedness, and selfishness. People trying to cover up, to control how information is released. I started this not knowing I was walking into a minefield."[11]

Yet Dr. Omalu continued to speak the truth. He felt he owed his candor to the professional football players who were afflicted with this terrible disease, and their wives and families.

In 2013, the NFL reached a $765 million settlement with the more than four thousand former football players who joined in a class-action lawsuit against the league for concealing the dangers of concussions and too quickly putting injured players back into play. The settlement was approved by a federal judge in 2015. In agreeing to the settlement, the NFL admitted no wrongdoing in the concussion saga. According to NFL executive vice president Jeffrey Pash, "We thought it was critical to get more help to players and families who deserve it than spend many years and millions of dollars on litigation."[12]

What the NFL's statement doesn't mention is that if it wasn't for the efforts of Dr. Bennet Omalu—the man whose complete surname, Onyemalukwube, in his native language means "If you know, come forth and speak"—there would have been no settlement, and the CTE epidemic among professional football players might never have come to light. Omalu says, "Before CTE, retired football players were ridiculed and dismissed. I think they're beginning to get the attention they need."[13]

And I would argue they're finally getting the attention they deserve.

Leadership Archetype: The Truth Teller

A moment of choice is a moment of truth.
It's the testing point of our character and
our competence.

—Stephen Covey

The truth teller strongly believes that he owes it to his people, customers, and communities to be open, sincere, and honest at all times. The truth teller will not hesitate to tell the truth, even if it means that his candor makes people uncomfortable. He speaks with openness and honesty, driven by a sincere desire to help, and the authentic intention to be of service to others. For truth tellers, speaking up is a duty. The truth teller always asks himself, **"Where should I speak up?"**

Being a truth teller and standing up against others for what is right is never easy. But to speak dishonestly is deeply conflicting for a truth teller, and so he instinctively avoids it. Even if on occasion telling the truth might hurt others, he believes wholeheartedly that, regardless of repercussions, it is always the right thing to do.

The Key to the Truth Teller's Success: Candor

Silence becomes cowardice when occasion demands speaking out the whole truth and acting accordingly.

—Mahatma Gandhi

Speaking with candor in everyday life is one of the hardest things we can do. According to research conducted at the University of Massachusetts, 60 percent of adults cannot complete a ten-minute conversation without lying at least once. The study also found that the people in the group of liars told an average of three lies during their ten-minute conversation.[14]

Most people say they want to hear the truth, but the fact that so many truth tellers have been punished for their actions proves differently. As the ancient proverb says, "If you tell the truth, have one foot in the stirrup." In other words, when you speak with candor, you should also be ready to suffer the consequences for telling it. Truth tellers know this to be the case, but it doesn't deter them.

While your mind rationalizes your tendency to lie, it is your heart that urges you to be honest and open.

When you speak with candor, you don't have to keep track of what you said to whom. And you avoid accidently contradicting yourself.

As a leader, when you tell lies, you have to keep a mental record of exactly what you told each person you deceived, and this can become tricky if you accidentally contradict yourself.

When you speak with candor, you earn the reputation of being a truthful person.

As a leader, you always want to be known as the person who speaks with candor. Sometimes people might not want to hear what you have to say, but it's better for them to know the truth than to be deceived.

When you tell the truth, people follow your example and are more truthful with *you*.

As a leader, if you tell those who follow you that you have failed many times before, your people will feel safe enough to tell you when *they* have failed.

As a leader, deceiving others can take a toll on your health, your relationships, and your career.

When you speak with candor, and when you are honest and open, your stress level drops, and you can sleep better, feel better, eat better, and look better. According to research conducted by University of Notre Dame psychology professor Anita Kelly, those committed to telling the truth—even for small things—reported significantly fewer physical health symptoms than a control group. They felt less tense, and they had fewer sore throats, nausea, and headaches.[15]

When you tell the truth, it causes you to feel self-confidence and pride; when you deceive, it causes you to feel depressed and self-critical.

When you tell the truth, you are more persuasive and believable. To be believable, you must always speak up with candor—you must always tell the truth.

As a leader, people are watching you, so what you say and what you do has to be filled with truth and candor. Your leadership style must be that of a truth teller.

The foundation of candor lies within those who tell the truth. When we speak with candor . . .

We create compelling companies.

We create effective leadership.

We create loyal, engaged employees.

We create competitive advantage.

We create ethical workplaces.

We create cultures of integrity.

Be someone whom others can depend on to tell the truth and speak with candor, regardless of the circumstances.

The Truth Teller's Leadership Gap: Suspicion

The moment there is suspicion about a
person's motive, everything he does becomes
tainted.

—Mahatma Gandhi

Deborah was a young CFO who was successful, smart, and
serious. She was extremely well versed in the finances of the
company, and knew exactly when to take risks—and when to
play it conservatively. Deborah excelled at her job, and the
company grew.

One day, the company's CEO announced that he was
going to retire at the end of the year, so the board let it be
known that they were looking for someone to replace the
CEO, and that they wanted to promote from within. After
interviewing a small selection of people—including two internal candidates—the board decided that Deborah was the
natural choice. And, so, without much fanfare, Deborah was
promoted to the CEO position of a successful and thriving
business.

At first, Deborah wasn't sure what it was that made her
the top choice for the board, but she figured that they had
recognized her hard work and dedication. She was happy to
be in this new position, and she was looking forward to the
board's support as she transitioned. Deborah was also a bit

nervous that she might not hit the ground running, but she was certain that—with the help of her great team—they would make it work and the company would succeed more than it ever had before.

One of the first jobs for the new CEO was to create a business plan for a new product line, and within a week she completed a solid draft. When Deborah presented her business plan to the board, she asked for resources to support the new product launch. The board was unanimous in its agreement, telling Deborah that they would give her what she needed.

Deborah left the meeting excited and eager to meet with the product team to start implementing her plans—she wanted to show the board just what she was capable of.

But not even a week later, the board came back to Deborah and, without explanation or clarification, told her they had changed their minds. Instead of giving her the funds she had requested in one lump sum, they told her she would have to ask for it as she needed it—and make a presentation to the entire board each time.

Deborah became enraged. She told her team behind closed doors that the board was filled with a bunch of liars. Soon the rage she felt at being deceived by the board began to have a negative effect on Deborah's demeanor in the office. Her team started to become wary of Deborah's constant ranting, and suspicion and paranoia became the order of the day.

The board realized that something was wrong, though they weren't sure what. They told Deborah in one of their weekly meetings to hire herself a coach. "You must work on being a leader," they told her.

When I first started to work with Deborah, I could tell she was angry about something, but I wasn't clear what the triggers were. She kept telling me her board was filled with liars. "They don't speak the truth," she said. Unclear about the circumstances, I asked her to explain.

She told me that a few months earlier she created a business plan for a new product and asked for the money necessary to launch it. The board signed off on it, and then a week later they said no to the money. "They are deceivers!" she screamed.

I asked Deborah to calm down. "I understand that you feel you have been lied to," I told her. "I hear you feel deceived."

But I kept wondering what the full story was—I had the distinct feeling that I was getting only her side of it. What led the board to say yes to Deborah in one meeting and then one week later tell her no?

When we are deceived, it can hurt like hell and it can make us angry. But it can also create a severe leadership gap by making us paranoid and suspicious of others. The board had their reasons, but they didn't bother to tell Deborah. And in not doing so, they turned a potentially great leader into a paranoid one.

For the first few weeks of our engagement, all Deborah wanted to talk about were the deceivers on the board and their vast dysfunction. I suggested we get on the phone with the board and ask them what happened, but she didn't want to do that. I next suggested we ask a specific board member—someone Deborah used to trust and respect—what had happened. She agreed to this, and a meeting was scheduled.

The day and time for the meeting arrived, and you could feel the tension in the air. My role was to listen and facilitate a conversation that I hoped would get us to the truth of what had actually happened. The goal was for each person to tell his or her side of the story, and Deborah went first. The tone of her voice was sincere, but her suspicion was palpable. "Why did you deceive me and why did the board lie to me?" she asked. "How can I succeed if I don't have the money I need for the new product launch?"

The board member looked at Deborah with amazement in his eyes. "We did not deceive you," he said fervently. "The reason we did not give you the funds all at once is because we needed to set aside part of it at the last minute for a stock buyback. There is money for you, but not at once—we just can't afford it right now."

"You mean we can still get all the money we need for the new product launch," Deborah asked, "just not all at once?"

"Yes, Deborah, we told you that at the board meeting," replied the board member.

Both were quiet.

While the board did not intentionally deceive Deborah, its members *did* withhold information from her—a trait that is common with many boards. In this case, deception took the form of a misunderstanding. The result was that Deborah *felt* she had been deceived, which caused her to become suspicious and paranoid. As a result, her leadership suffered.

Withholding information is worse than disclosing the truth—not only for ourselves but also for those we manage. If we feel others deceive us, we get suspicious. Suspicion is like a virus— once it infiltrates hearts and minds, it affects how we think, act, and lead.

If a truth teller succumbs to suspicion, the results can be disastrous.

The Truth Teller's Leadership Gap Archetype: The Deceiver

Men are so simple and so much inclined to
obey immediate needs that a deceiver will
never lack victims for his deception.
                              —Niccolò Machiavelli

The truth teller versus the deceiver is a leadership manifestation we know very well. We learn about deceivers in history, we hear stories about them in the news, and we meet them in our everyday lives. The world is filled with deceivers. On some level, perhaps, we're all deceivers. And surely we have all been deceived.

Here are the marks of an archetypal deceiver:

Remarkably charming. Deceivers know how to use charm to their advantage—they know how to get attention and keep it. Outright lying comes very easy to deceivers, and they can lie in the smoothest manner. They'll tell you the most implausible story—and you just believe it, even if something tells you it doesn't make sense. The most charming deceivers can get away with anything.

Emotionally manipulative. Often deceivers will ask you to choose sides or pressure you to say you trust them. Though deceivers are never to be trusted, they have a way of getting you to question yourself.

Wonderful at distraction. Deceivers can change the subject with great finesse. You may start a conversation on one topic, and before you know it you are talking about something else. Or they distract you from what really needs to be discussed by using body language, like smiling or leaning in closer, as if they are telling you a secret.

Notorious blamers. Deceivers never take accountability or responsibility. Instead, they find someone convenient to blame.

Professional bait and switchers. Deceivers may convince you that you have their commitment or support, but when there is a minor change in conditions, or some fine-print terms aren't met, they create an out. The truth is you never had their commitment.

Leverage the Deceiver Within

> The trouble with lying and deceiving is that their efficiency depends entirely upon a clear notion of the truth that the liar and deceiver wishes to hide.
>
> —Hannah Arendt

Lies and deception follow us from birth to death, sometimes seeping into every corner of our communication and every crevice of our relationships both private and public. We want to believe that lying is bad, yet we teach and train deception. So, if everyone lies and deceives, why is it still a shock to us when it happens, even when the deceivers are people we were certain could be relied on for the truth?

Truth tellers must speak up, and those who feel deceived must speak up, too. This is the only way to get to the bottom of a situation and clear out suspicion. We may not always like what we hear, but at least we will know the truth.

Here are some ways to confront the deceiver within you:

Don't let pride get the best of you. Sometimes you become a deceiver because there are parts of you that feel inadequate, insecure, or even vulnerable, and they cause you great shame. This can make you cover it all up with a whole bunch of lies. But you don't have to let your pride get the best of you. Who you are—weaknesses and all—should be okay. If not, use your feelings to change your direction and make things different. Don't let your pride get the best of you, and work on bringing out the best parts of who you are.

Stop obscuring the truth. Self-deception obscures the truth about you; it corrupts your view of others and your own circumstances, and it inhibits your ability to make wise and helpful decisions. Stop hiding from the truth. Because the truth is your future, your future may depend on how well you manage to preserve a commitment to the truth in the face of all the deception around you. Ask yourself why you need to deceive, what gains you get, and if it is really worth it.

Admit when you are not telling the truth. Many people have a hard time admitting that they are wrong, so they continue lying and deceiving. But the power isn't in lying; it's in the truth. And as a deceiver you ultimately have to choose. Despite what you think you know, you have to admit you *don't* know, and that is okay. You are not perfect—you are an imperfect human with an imperfect brain—but you can still decide to respect truth and the process for establishing it. Benjamin Franklin famously made a point of admitting when he was wrong, because he believed that by hearing out those he disagreed with he reduced his fear of being wrong.

Learn to be flexible. People who tend to deceive see the world in black and white. They have this rigidity to them about what is right or wrong, fact or fiction; and they are always drawing a line in the sand. But life doesn't work that way. Nothing is all of this and nothing of that. As a human being, your inflexibility can lead to your failure. As people who have a tendency to use deception, we should leverage and rise above our shortcomings, learning to start again with more flexibility and agility.

When you can admit instead of hide what makes you feel ashamed, vulnerable, or inadequate, you are one step closer to achieving greatness from within.

Becoming a Truth Teller Leader

I must continue to bear testimony to truth even if I am forsaken by all. Mine may today be a voice in the wilderness, but it will be heard when all other voices are silenced, if it is the voice of Truth.

—Mahatma Gandhi

Great leaders are honest and speak with candor. People respect those who tell the truth, even when the truth is difficult to swallow. Honest hearts produce honest actions. For many of us, it seems impossible to always be honest and tell the truth, but there is a way to increase candor and reduce deception. Here's how you can do it:

Work on being a truth teller. Everything that is meaningful starts with a great leader. When there is a lack of truth in an organization, it starts at the top. Honest leaders, the leaders who are truth tellers, cultivate a culture of candor. Otherwise people are driven by mistrust, misgivings, and misunderstandings. Most of all, they are driven by fear—and when fear is present, lying begins. Make honesty an implicit value, but remember that it will mean nothing unless you and other leaders in your organization model and demonstrate truthfulness in your leadership.

Communicate everything—don't hold back. Communicate, communicate, communicate, and hold nothing back. Unless there is a specific, honest reason for not sharing information, employees should be told *everything* of importance to them. Managers who keep saying they have a culture of candor but aren't truly transparent will demolish trust and create suspicion in their organization. Don't be the kind of leader who allows rumors to fester and gossip to grow. Be the kind of leader who communicates and engages.

Create a culture of candor and solutions. Instead of blaming your employees when things go wrong, look for solutions. People should feel free to make mistakes, because it is a normal part of a person's growth and development, and it will also prevent them from lying to cover up mistakes in the future. Cultivate a culture of candor, in which owning up to your mistakes is okay and it is safe to fail publicly. The best way we can lead our people is to provide them with the sufficient resources they need—from budget, to people, to time—to help them actually do the job that is required. Then they won't have to make excuses for not being on time or for not reaching their goals.

Eliminate barricades of insufficiencies. Get rid of the roadblocks that keep people from performing, and do all that you can to eliminate policies and principles that create liars.

If you advocate honesty, don't punish the messenger. If you ask for candor, don't discipline the truth teller.

Treat everyone equally. The cultures that thrive are the cultures that continually treat everyone the same. Don't let people feel as though they are against one another; make them feel they are important. Don't play favorites, and don't reward suck-ups. Every employee should be responsible for what he says and how he says it. You want to foster a culture of candor in which everyone is willing to speak with honesty.

Model your own high standards. Do all that you can to let others know that you will not hire or tolerate liars, deceivers, and cheats. Keep your standards high, and do everything you can to reach them daily. Make truth a consistent part of your own leadership and your business.

Give them reasons to be better. Don't allow your team to be pessimistic. Give your company and your people something to develop and grow toward. Let people know they are part of something bigger than themselves. Provide them with a vision and a path for getting there, and then reward them for being truth tellers and for speaking with candor.

GREAT TRUTH-TELLING LEADERS

Ronald Reagan was not afraid to speak his mind, whether it was about the dangers of the Soviet empire or the importance of reforming the tax code. Whether you agreed with him or not, you could respect him for speaking the truth.

Indra Nooyi has taken flack for speaking her mind and saying that a woman who is a CEO for a company with the size and reach of PepsiCo can't have it all. Nooyi said, "Stay at home mothering was a full time job. Being a CEO for a company is three full time jobs rolled into one. How can you do justice to it all?"

Winston Churchill helped guide the British people to victory against the Nazis by consistently telling them the unvarnished truth about their dire situation in World War II. It was said that he could tell his followers the worst, hurling it to them like great hunks of bleeding meat.

Truth tellers are the most unique archetype, and probably the most misunderstood. When they speak up with candor, they are not out to harm people—rather, they are driven by a strong sense of justice and by a deep, compelling desire to do the right thing.

When truth tellers see deception and lies, or experience injustice, or witness pain being inflicted on others, they feel they must say and do something.

For truth tellers, being truthful is not a choice. It is a deep calling.

Recognizing Yourself in the Truth Teller Archetype

The truth teller speaks with candor and is not afraid to speak the truth against injustice, lying, or greed.

Are you a truth teller? Ask yourself these questions:

- In what ways is speaking with candor important to you?

- What would cause you to speak up?

- In what cases would you intentionally evade the truth?

- When do you think it's okay to lie or mislead?

- When should you be outspoken?

CHAPTER FIVE

THE HERO

The hero is fearless. He doesn't hesitate to act while others stand by.

If I asked you to write down the names of ten great businesspeople—men and women who forever changed the course of the world through their actions—chances are Henry Ford would be somewhere on your list. Everyone has heard the story of the famous man who founded the car company that bore his name, and who is credited with designing one of the most important innovations of the Industrial Age—the moving assembly line. And everyone has heard the story of the creation of the affordable and reliable Model T automobile, which enabled everyday Americans to travel wherever there were roads to take them.

By 1914, sales of the car passed the 250,000 mark, with the price for the basic touring model dropping to just $360 by

1916, when sales reached 472,000 units. Ford so dominated the industry that one-half of all automobiles in the United States were Ford Model Ts. However, for all of Henry Ford's talents, and all of his success, he was a deeply flawed man.

In 1918, Henry turned over the day-to-day operations of the Ford Motor Company to his son, Edsel, who was named president. However, despite this change in company leadership, Henry retained authority to make the final decisions about important company matters, and so Edsel had little real authority to make any sort of important decisions in the company that he led at least by title.

Ultimately, Henry's flaws caught up with him, and the Ford Motor Company suffered significant financial damage as a result. It would take a hero to rescue the business— someone with a tremendous reservoir of courage. Surprisingly, this hero would turn out to be Edsel.

Edsel Ford—Henry and Clara Ford's only child—was born in 1893, and unlike his father, he enjoyed a life of privilege. When he was young, he tinkered on cars with his famous father, but his interests shifted to design as he matured. He attended private schools and enjoyed painting, photography, and sports.

Edsel Ford wasn't like his father. He was educated, he was worldly, he was young, and he had style. According to historian Steven Watts, "Henry was, in many ways, a farmer's son. He was very old-fashioned. He was barely educated."[1] On the other hand, continues Watts, "Edsel Ford [was] a very kind-hearted, genteel, quiet young man." When Edsel decided to build a new wing on the company's administration building to relieve overcrowding—going so far as to have the foundations dug—Henry overruled him, deciding that the extra employee space was an unnecessary luxury. And when Edsel told his father he would have the holes for the foundation filled with dirt, returning the grounds to their original state, again his father overruled him. Henry wanted a visible reminder to Edsel of his ultimate power over the Ford Motor Company, and over Edsel, who commented to a friend about the incident, "I don't know what kick Father gets out of humiliating me this way."

Despite the phenomenal success of Henry Ford's Model T, by the 1920s the car was getting long in the tooth. After sales of the Model T had reached a remarkable 10 million units, the car's market share then dipped below 50 percent as consumers turned their attention to exciting new products from other manufacturers. Alfred Sloan—the progressive CEO of General Motors—realized that consumers wanted *more* than a car that was inexpensive, sturdy, and reliable, and that would take them from Point A to Point B. They increasingly wanted a car that would take them there *in style*—even if it cost them more money. And the Model T was beginning to look like last year's model.

Edsel Ford and other key members of the Ford leadership team could see that change was needed—and fast—but Henry Ford was adamant against producing a replacement for his beloved Model T, which he considered to be "the most perfect car in the world." When Edsel found out that the Lincoln Motor Company—which had been started in 1917 by one of the founders of Cadillac—was having financial trouble, Edsel lobbied his father hard to buy the ailing brand. Eventually, Henry Ford relented, and in 1922 Lincoln was acquired by Ford. Edsel then focused on developing Lincoln into Ford's first luxury-car brand.

But that still wasn't enough to turn the tide in Ford's fortunes.

In a January 1926 memo to Henry Ford, Ford vice president Ernest Kanzler wrote, "Our Ford customers are going to other manufacturers. . . . With every additional car our competitors sell, they get stronger and we get weaker. . . . A new product is necessary." Henry Ford was not at all pleased by the memo, and Kanzler was gone within just a few months.

But Edsel, who agreed with Kanzler's candid assessment, courageously refused to back down. According to Steven Watts, "Edsel became convinced that times had changed, consumers had become more sophisticated, and you simply needed to put a new model out there."[2] Edsel fought with his father for more than a year—showing up in Henry's office to press his position, sometimes carrying plans for new cars with him. Each time, Henry sent him away.

If not for Edsel Ford, however, the company that bears his and his father's name might not exist today. Despite his father's continued protests, Edsel finally convinced him to completely rethink the future of the Ford automobile. To compete successfully in the fast-evolving automobile market would require that consumers be given choices, styling options, and new ways to finance their purchases. Edsel knew this to be the case, and only by continually taking on and finally convincing his father—a man revered as one of the greatest businessmen in history—was the company able to change with the times. As a Ford colleague recalled, "It was the old man's belief that he knew best what was good for [the public]. Edsel, on the other hand, would try to give the public what they wanted."[3]

In May 1926, as the 15 millionth Model T rolled off the assembly line, the Ford Motor Company announced that it would stop production of the car. In its stead would be an "entirely new Ford car," styled and designed by Edsel Ford. This car turned out to be the sleek, new Model A, which sold 700,000 units in its first year and turned around Ford's sales decline—saving the company from ruin. Regardless, Henry Ford never forgave Edsel for pushing him to kill the Model T.

Edsel Ford was the hero who courageously saved the Ford Motor Company. He had all the luxuries imaginable—wealth, family, and a position as president of the greatest automobile company in the world. But he was willing to put it all on the line to save the company that bore his name. He was heroic when the Ford Motor Company most needed a hero.

Maybe we should turn the conventional wisdom about Henry Ford's story on its head and consider who the *real* hero was—which man should have been hailed as one of the true greats of American business and the automobile industry.

Like Edsel, a hero takes courageous actions when no one else is ready to step in.

Despite his repeated efforts to push his son, Edsel, out of the picture, Henry Ford—and his beloved company—were ultimately saved by Edsel. If the brilliant but stubborn Henry Ford would have had his way, his beloved Model T might have been the last car the Ford Motor Company ever produced. And if Henry Ford would have had his way, would the Ford Motor Company still be around today? Perhaps not.

We live in a world that enables us to think we know it all. But that leaves us inarticulate in our thinking; it makes us stubborn and headstrong, and it sets us up for failure. The truth is we don't know what we don't know. To be a successful leader, we have to at times be courageous enough to say, "This is not working." And we have to be heroic enough to say, "I might not know the answers, but I will try anyway."

Few at the Ford Motor Company were willing to challenge Henry Ford. The most important among those few was his son, Edsel. If not for the heroic—courageous, constant, and gentle—persuasive manner of Edsel Ford, the company might have ended up as just a footnote in the history of the American automobile industry, or just a division of General Motors. The truth is that the decision to make a new model car to replace the Model T was not Henry's; it was Edsel's.

Who designed it?

Edsel.

Who made sure it got done?

Edsel.

Who was the courageous one and the *real* hero of the Ford Motor Company?

Edsel.

Leadership Archetype: The Hero

A hero is an ordinary individual who finds
the strength to persevere and endure in spite
of overwhelming obstacles.

—Christopher Reeve

When others stand on the sidelines, waiting for someone to step up, heroes are the ones who don't hesitate to act. Heroes are *courageous*—they are willing to put their careers at risk for a shot at greatness.

Heroes act when others of lesser courage will not.

Heroes act in spite of fear and overwhelming opposition.

Most of us are not really afraid of being brave—we are afraid of what it takes to be brave. Heroes consistently ask themselves, **"Where is courage needed?"**

The Key to the Hero's Success: Courage

Courage is resistance to fear, mastery of
fear, not absence of fear.

—Mark Twain

We are not really afraid of losing everything—we are afraid of what will happen when we have nothing. When you understand what you are afraid of, you can learn what it means to be courageous. When we dilute our fear, we strengthen our courage and our courage strengthens us.

Courage has been found to originate deep within the brain. Researchers led by Dr. Yadin Dudai at the Weizmann Institute of Science in Rehovot, Israel, used fMRI scans of experiment volunteers to determine that a particular part of the brain—the subgenual anterior cingulate cortex (sgACC), an area extremely rich in serotonin transporters—was activated when the subjects behaved heroically. Dr. Dudai says, "Our results propose an account for brain processes and mechanisms supporting an intriguing aspect of human behavior, the ability to carry out a voluntary action opposite to that promoted by ongoing fear, namely courage."[4]

According to the work of University of Houston researcher Brené Brown, we are driven to lead fear-based lives when we believe in our own unworthiness. Brown says, "Daring greatly is about showing up and being seen. It's about owning our vulnerability and understanding it as the birthplace of courage and the other meaningful experiences in our lives."[5]

Philip Zimbardo is professor emeritus of psychology at Stanford University, a former president of the American Psychological Association, and founder and president of the Heroic Imagination Project. According to Zimbardo, "When we ask why people become heroic, research doesn't yet have an answer. It could be that heroes have more compassion or empathy; maybe there's a hero gene; maybe it's because of their levels of oxytocin. . . . We don't know for sure."[6]

According to Zimbardo's research, heroism is an activity that has four different and distinct characteristics:

- It is performed in service to others in need, or in defense of certain ideals.

- It is engaged in voluntarily.

- It is performed with the recognition of possible risks and costs—to one's physical health or personal reputation—in which the person is willing to accept anticipated sacrifice.

- It is performed without external gain anticipated at the time of the act.

As with every archetype there are two sides to the coin, but it's not as simple as who is bad and who is good, what is evil and what is not. Rather, we must challenge the idea of who is a hero and who is not, what it means to be courageous and what it means to be cowardly, and what distinguishes the brave from the fearless.

The Hero's Leadership Gap: Fear

> Fear defeats more people than anything in the world.
>
> —Ralph Waldo Emerson

We've all heard stories of leaders—in business and in history—who stand on the sidelines and watch as their organizations and people suffer demise. This passive behavior is stunning to those who witness it. It is perplexing that a once passionate leader could stand idly by and give up. Are they not true leaders among us? Why can't they manage crises? Have they lost their belief in their mission? The simple answer is that fear is paralyzing.

No matter what the root source of the leader's fear is, the effect of fear on an organization can be devastating.

The Hero's Leadership Gap Archetype: The Bystander

> The world will not be destroyed by those who do evil, but by those who watch them without doing anything.
>
> —Albert Einstein

Terry was a very talented and skilled man in a position of great responsibility, but for some reason he was unwilling to step up and lead his people and his organization. He practiced what I call *leadership by osmosis*—he expected his people to lead themselves with no support or direction. This turned out to be a seriously unrealistic expectation on his part.

People are inspired by great leaders—they are more committed and more engaged in their jobs, and they perform better. Bad leaders turn organizations upside-down. Employee turnover increases, people become disengaged in their jobs, and performance suffers—resulting in very real short- and long-term damage.

My assignment was to help Terry resist being a bystander, and become an engaged and effective leader as his organization fell apart all around him. But the moment I first met him, I knew this was going to be a tremendous challenge. I could see he was not good at dealing with people—he enjoyed dealing with the various processes and practices in the business far more than he enjoyed dealing with the people. He loved saying, "Give me a process and I will make it work." He had risen up the ranks of the organization by doing what was asked of him. And until now, he had never held a leadership role.

When he was promoted, Terry was asked to deliver on audacious goals. But in truth he had no clue how to deliver the goals he had agreed to, because Terry was, by nature, a manager. He valued control, systems, numbers, spreadsheets, and structure. Terry was not about inspiring the people who worked for him, he was not about creating trust with others, and he really didn't know how to build a team that could attain the lofty goals his board had set for him.

This, of course, became a huge problem—for him and for the company—especially when decisions needed to be made. Instead of weighing the alternatives and taking decisive action, he preferred to avoid dealing with situations—allowing things to work out the way they did, good or bad. In truth, his lack of leadership was losing his company money, and costing him his success.

This outcome, of course, wasn't entirely his fault. The company's board had chosen Terry over a very talented group of candidates. They wanted to reward him for his loyalty to the company, and trusted he would rise to the occasion. But when he didn't become the kind of leader they had hoped for, the board called me in to help.

We had many discussions on what needed to change, but Terry kept insisting that strong leadership was not his style. He would rather work on the nuts and bolts of processes and practices and procedures. "The moment I get the right process in place," he told me, "everything and everyone will come together."

I brought my concerns about Terry's reticence to lead to the board, and they were even more insistent. "Just get him into shape," I was told.

I responded, "There's nothing to get into shape if someone is not willing to change."

It was no surprise to me that Terry was ultimately unable to deliver on the goals the board had set for him and that the program failed. He had chosen to be a bystander when his people and his organization needed a hero—someone who would courageously lead the way. But Terry wasn't done yet. Instead of accepting responsibility for the failure of the program, he consciously made the situation worse by blaming his people for his *own* failures. He threw his team under the bus

and blamed them for lacking commitment and accountability.

It was bad enough that he took no personal responsibility
for his leadership mistakes. But it quickly became crystal
clear that being a bystander and lacking the courage to stand
up for his team as everything was falling apart was a big part
of why he was an ineffective leader.

A few months later, the team was still there, but Terry
was out of a job.

After Terry was dismissed, the board gave me the assignment of picking up the pieces and making the leadership team
whole again. This was no easy task—it took quite some time
for the toxic residue left by Terry's leadership to work its way
out of the organization. People were hurt and scarred from
their brush with a boss who was a bystander and who lacked
courage. But with the incentive of bringing understanding to
their experience, not only were we able to succeed, but we sur-
passed the expectations of many.

We accomplished this in four specific steps. First, we acknowledged and named the elephant in the room—allowing
people to speak up without fear or negative repercussions.
Second, we neutralized the blame game—explaining that it
was more important to move forward than to look back.
Third, we rallied people together as a community. Finally, we
kept the team moving forward by providing them with a
compelling vision and purposeful mission.

When you witness a tragedy, or when you hear about an
injustice, or when you see someone bullying another, what do

you do? Do you speak up or do you remain silent? Do you offer help or do you walk away?

There is a fine line between those who stand by and those who speak up.

The ones who speak up are courageous, and we hail them as heroes. Then there are those who do nothing, and we call them bystanders.

The bystander effect is the tendency for individuals in a group to avoid taking heroic action when other group members don't take heroic action themselves. According to researchers, the more people there are in a group, the greater the tendency of the individuals in it to act as bystanders.

To explore the psychological effects of becoming a prisoner or prison guard, in 1971, Philip Zimbardo and his team of researchers designed a project known as the Stanford Prison Experiment. The team placed a classified ad in a local newspaper looking for volunteers.

MALE COLLEGE STUDENTS NEEDED FOR PSYCHOLOGICAL STUDY OF PRISON LIFE. $15 PER DAY FOR 1–2 WEEKS.[7]

More than seventy volunteers came forward, and this pool of applicants was narrowed down to a final group of twenty-four study participants. Zimbardo and his research team randomly assigned each participant one of two roles—that of prisoner or guard. Ultimately, twelve participants were designated to be prisoners, and twelve participants to be guards.

The young men selected to participate in the experiment

as prisoners were "arrested" at their homes by real Palo Alto police officers, booked at the police station, and brought to a mock jail in the basement of Jordan Hall at Stanford University. It was there that they would be imprisoned for a period of up to fourteen days. The prisoners experienced much of the things a normal prisoner goes through, from wearing prison uniforms to being subjected to mandatory strip searches and solitary confinement.

The subjects who played the role of guard in the mock prison were told to think of themselves as *real* prison guards in a *real* prison. While they were instructed not to mistreat the prisoners or cause them any physical harm, they were also told to let the prisoners know who was in charge. Zimbardo gave the guards this briefing:

> You can create in the prisoners feelings of boredom, a sense of fear to some degree, you can create a notion of arbitrariness that their life is totally controlled by us, by the system, you, me. . . . They can do nothing, say nothing that we don't permit.[8]

To make the guards look more authentic, they were dressed in khaki uniforms and issued wooden batons to signify their authority. As Zimbardo said, the goal was to induce disorientation, depersonalization, and deindividualization in the participants; and the participants quickly took to their assigned roles.

The first day everything was fine and the prisoners were bored and quiet. However, on the second day, there was a major shift when some of the prisoners started a revolt against the prison guards. In response, some of the guards began to take their roles very seriously and became extremely cruel. They enforced authoritative measures on the prisoners that were sadistic, and some even subjected their prisoners to psychological torture. Many of the prisoners passively accepted the abuse, and those who tried to prevent it were harassed and punished.

This went on for six days, until Zimbardo abruptly terminated the experiment due to the rampant abuses. Dave Eshelman, who played the role of a guard in the experiment, said,

> I was kind of running my own experiment in there, by saying, "How far can I push these things and how much abuse will these people take before they say, 'knock it off'?" But the other guards didn't stop me. They seemed to join in. They were taking my lead. Not a single guard said, "I don't think we should do this."[9]

The Stanford Prison Experiment has received much criticism over the years, but it continues to raise questions even today. How is it possible that good people turn into perpetrators? Why do people who have power become evil? And why do some have a tendency to turn a blind eye and a deaf ear on actions that may be abusive?

These are important questions.

During World War II, Nazi military officers ordered the death of millions of Jews and other "undesirables" (Gypsies, communists, homosexuals, the mentally and physically disabled, and others) while those who knew stood by—watching as bystanders.

We don't have to go to the extremes of war, and we don't need to create a mock prison experiment to see the bystander effect in action. All we have to do is go into our own workplace and look at our leadership.

Research on workplace bullying revealed that 66.6 percent of businesses have an active bully—with 58.2 percent of participants stating that the active bully was more likely to be a boss (manager, senior manager, CEO, or executive director).[10] Bullying at work is a huge problem, and sadly, many who witness bullying won't say or do anything about it—instead, they act as bystanders. They might excuse the bullying by saying, "Oh this always goes on," or "He was only teasing," or "This bullying salesperson brings us too much business to be reprimanded." The fact is that when bullying or intimidation occurs in the workplace, many people just stand by and watch. Most people believe that someone else will handle it, or that the people being bullied can take care of themselves. When nothing is done to help a coworker when he or she is being bullied, this is the bystander effect in action.

Are we going to be one of the people who stand by and allow toxic behaviors to continue to exist, or are we going to be one of the heroes who takes a courageous stand? There is an opportunity every day, in every workplace, in every organization, for the courageous hero archetype to emerge and to lead.

Leveraging the Bystander Within

And thou shalt never, but never be a
bystander.

—Yehuda Bauer

Leaders do not become *true* leaders until they can learn to manage their fears in the face of difficulties and challenges. True leaders have worked diligently and with great effort to go beyond what they fear and to rethink what they know, so they can discover within themselves a depth of their own fearlessness—the person who is ready to be courageous like never before.

If you want your people to be courageous (and you do), then you as a leader need to rethink your organization's culture and ask yourself if it supports and encourages acts of courage, both great and small.

To have a culture that is courageous, you have to find the hero within. It's the hero who takes back control from fear. The hero says, "I will find the courage to do what I know I am capable of, even though I don't yet know how."

To find the hero within, you have to make it safe for people to be courageous by cushioning their fall. You do that by allowing people to be themselves. Because when you make it safe for people to be themselves, you make it safe for them to take chances and to take risks. In a culture where safety resides, *everyone* flourishes. When people feel safe, they risk big, and when they don't feel safe, they avoid doing anything that might point the finger of blame on them if they make a mistake or fail. The safer your people feel, the more your business will achieve as the climate of fear evaporates.

To leverage your inner bystander . . .

When you see something, do something. Bystanders have a knack of not wanting to get involved, but as someone who is looking to be brave, courageous, and fearless, make a point of intervening as soon as you even think there may be a problem. Don't brush it off as "this is how it always is." If you hear disrespect, say something; if you see misconduct, do something. All questionable behavior should be addressed immediately to keep a situation from escalating. Your purpose is not to watch things pass you by; your purpose is to see something and do something about it.

Implement an intervention for yourself. How many times have you said to yourself, "It is what it is"? It is your job to stop idly standing by as your day-to-day life continues not to be the way you want it to be. Instead of playing the bystander role, put a plan in motion to change what needs to be changed in order for you to be happy and successful.

End your own passivity. You are in control of your own life and your own happiness to a huge extent. If success is going to find you, you have to be brave and assertive *now*— not tomorrow, later, next week, or next month. Your bravery, fearlessness, and courage have to start today—you cannot just stand by and wish for it to happen. You have to be the one who makes it happen. No one is going to come and rescue you or fix things for you.

Be the person you know you can be. Being a bystander in your own life doesn't benefit you, so don't be a bystander in others' lives either. Learn to exercise more empathy, and let someone know you are there for them, to help them, guide them, and support them if they need you. Don't make assumptions—not everyone is as courageous or as fearless as you are. Be the person you know you can be and stop just standing by and allowing life to pass you by.

The moment you choose not to be a bystander is the moment you uncover the hero within.

Becoming a Heroic Leader

Hard times don't create heroes. It is during the hard times when the "hero" within us is revealed.

—Bob Riley

What makes someone a great leader and a hero to others? To be a great leader, you have to lead your people in a heroic and courageous way. Being a hero actually means being a servant to something bigger than you. Focusing on the greater good of the organization and your people, instead of focusing only on your own needs, will reap massive rewards.

The word *hero* is related to the Latin word *servo,* which means to serve. Great leaders aren't just heroes; they're also servants—to their people, their customers, their communities, and the world at large. People who think they are going to lead by demand or by hierarchy will lead only for a short time. But when you lead as a hero—with a servant heart—and you do so courageously, and with the goal of having people work toward something greater than themselves, you can accomplish any goals you set for yourself and your organization.

Courage is needed across the board—in leaders, cultures, teams, and companies.

You have courageous leadership when people trust your decisions instead of silently resisting your every move.

You have a courageous culture when employees raise the red flag on projects that are going south instead of hiding issues until they build into full-blown catastrophes.

You have a courageous team when employees come to you with remedies to problems they are facing, instead of dumping problems in your lap.

You have a courageous company when your people are candid and engaged during status meetings, instead of politely nodding their heads every time you speak.

Most of us don't spend time thinking about whether our business culture, leadership, and company are courageous and grooming heroes. This is a mistake, and the loss of a tremendous opportunity. When you have a courageous cul-ture, and heroic leadership, you'll see people trying new things outside their skill sets, deliberately seeking out leader-ship opportunities, and offering ideas for expanding the team's reach. When you have a courageous culture, you'll also cultivate engagement, motivation, and commitment among your people.

A heroic leader will stand up. Courageous leaders go through life knowing that there will be people who want to put them down and who will want them to fail. But they do their job with excellence despite the discouragement.

A heroic leader will stand out. Courageous leaders know that not everyone will be interested in what they have to say. They speak up anyway, and refuse to become invisible.

A heroic leader will stand tall. Science says standing tall with your legs and arms stretched wide conveys a sense of power and decreases stress. Researchers at Harvard and Co-lumbia Universities have shown that practicing the "power pose" for a few minutes increases testosterone and lowers cor-tisol, the stress hormone.

A heroic leader will stay calm. Courageous leaders know that when things get tough and emotions are on edge, not everything has to be said. Calm does not mean weak; calm means you are credible.

A heroic leader will not hedge. Courageous leaders are decisive—they know what they stand for and what they want. They don't say "I think so" or "I guess so." They speak with au-thority, they know what needs to be said, and they say it. Heroes are defined by their courage to stay focused and determined.

Those who inspire others are heroes.

Those who use their time wisely are heroes.

Those who love a lifetime of learning are heroes.

Those who nurture their passion with courage are heroes.

Those who become positively deviant are heroes.

Those who take on courageous acts on a daily basis are heroes.

GREAT COURAGEOUS LEADERS

Justice Anthony Kennedy is the deciding vote on many Supreme Court cases. His courage to follow his conscience on a variety of hotly debated political issues stands out in the court of public opinion.

Malala Yousafzai spoke out against the oppressiveness of denying education to girls in Pakistan and paid dearly for it. Yet she continues to speak out in determination to achieve her goals.

J. K. Rowling was destitute and without options, but she had an idea and the courage to relentlessly pursue it even though it was a long shot. She persevered in spite of constant rejection, and she has sold more than 400 million copies of her books.

Become a hero by being courageous, and make a commitment to challenge all that is wrong in whatever form it takes—doing so with moral courage linked to righteous character.

Let the most valued private virtues of courage and compassion be your guiding light regardless of whether or not you feel ready. Be heroic in thought and action.

Develop a personal code of honor that you can live by proudly every day and that you are willing to share with others.

Heroism is acting in service to others and on behalf of others. Heroism can be developed, can be taught, and can be trained—like other vital individual characteristics. To be a hero requires a sociocentric orientation rather than an egocentric one, because everyone has the capacity to be courageous.

Anyone can learn how to be courageous.

And everyone can make a difference.

Including *you*.

Recognizing Yourself in the Hero Archetype

The hero embarks on a courageous quest to perform a remarkable action, and in doing so overcomes obstacles—often putting the welfare of others before his own.

Are you a hero? Ask yourself these questions:

- In what ways do you face fear despite your struggles?

- How do you display boldness as a leader—and encourage others to be bold?

- What are some examples of your willingness to try new things?

- What would you do differently if you had nothing to fear?

- Do you ever worry that you are a bystander? Why or why not?

CHAPTER SIX

THE INVENTOR

*The inventor is a visionary, constantly innovating and
improving processes and products. The integrity of
his ideas is paramount, and he refuses to
settle for anything less than excellence.*

Today sushi is available in most major cities around the
world and many smaller ones, too. You can easily find it
in grocery stores, the big-box aisles of Costco, 7-Eleven, and
of course sushi bars. Sushi as we know it today originated in
Japan, where it was widely viewed for centuries as a snack
food, most often sold to busy people from stalls on the street
and quickly eaten by hand like hot dogs in New York City.
For most of its existence, the sushi industry never aspired to
be much. But that once laid-back attitude has changed dramatically.

The Ginza is a district in the city of Tokyo that looks,
feels, and smells like the love child of Times Square and Rodeo

Drive, with an added dash of Las Vegas glitz. The area is a hodgepodge of high-fashion boutiques, department stores, hostess clubs, automobile showrooms, restaurants, bars, art galleries, and theaters. And when night arrives, flashing neon signs and huge video screens create a raucous multicolored lightshow that rivals any in the world.

But away from all of the lights, take a fifteen-minute walk from the fabled Tsukiji fish market and go along the busy Harumi Dori, parallel with the Tokyo Metro Hibiya Line. A few blocks after you cross the Ginza's main shopping thoroughfare, Chuo Dori, take the stairs on your left that lead deep into the underground Ginza subway station. Find your way through the busy station (more than 250,000 passengers use the station on an average day) until you reach exit C6. Pass through the set of twin glass doors with gold lettering, and in just seconds, you will find yourself outside the entrance of a tiny restaurant called Sukiyabashi Jiro.

Though you'd never guess by its location, hidden in the basement of a subway station, Sukiyabashi Jiro is widely considered to be the best sushi restaurant in the world. Reservations for its ten seats are extremely hard to get—you'll need to reserve months in advance—and the price bears no reflection whatsoever to the ambience or humble beginnings of the restaurant's featured dish. The current price for the twenty-course *omakase* (chef's choice) menu is a steep 32,000 yen, about $275—per person.

How does a tiny, subterranean sushi joint draw aficionados from all around the world and earn a coveted rating of three Michelin stars eight years in a row—an honor that puts it in the rarefied stratosphere of the very best of the best restaurants worldwide, regardless of cuisine?

The secret is a ninety-one-year-old man who has dedicated his life to mastering the art of making sushi. When Jiro Ono was just seven years old, his family—who desperately needed the extra income—sent Jiro to a restaurant where he would both live and work. Jiro says, "I was too young to apprentice with the gardener or carpenter. The local restaurant was the only place that would take me. So that's how I ended up in this business."[1]

Sushi is so ingrained in Jiro's life, his heart, and his soul that when he sleeps, he dreams about it. Even at his age, Jiro is still coming up with new techniques and new approaches that he can try out in his restaurant to continue to up his game. Jiro says in the documentary *Jiro Dreams of Sushi,* "I do the same thing over and over, improving bit by bit. There is always a yearning to achieve more. I'll continue to climb, trying to reach the top, but no one knows where the top is."[2]

Jiro is an inventor who climbed to the very pinnacle of his profession by refusing to compromise his creations and by defending the integrity of his ideas.

Like many remarkable, creative people around the world, Jiro refuses to produce anything that doesn't meet his extremely high standards. He accomplishes this in five different ways.

First, Jiro became a specialist. In the early days of Suki-yabashi Jiro, the restaurant sold many dishes besides sushi. Then Jiro realized that people were filling up on appetizers and other food offerings, and by the time they reached the sushi course at the end of their visit, they would have room for only a few pieces. That's when Jiro decided to focus 100 percent on sushi. Order the omakase at Sukiyabashi Jiro, and you will receive exactly nineteen pieces of sushi and a dessert item at the end, typically a particularly flavorful and juicy slice of melon. While the sushi you'll be served changes from day to day—depending on which seafood is the best on offer at the market that day—every piece has the chef's full focus.

Second, Jiro found the very best vendors of the very best ingredients that he buys each day. For example, he built a long-term relationship with the vendor of a particular kind of rice, which Jiro considers to be the very best in the world and perfectly suited to his sushi. The relationship Jiro has with the rice vendor is so loyal that the vendor will not sell this special strain of rice to anyone else without Jiro's explicit approval. Similarly, when Jiro's son Yoshikazu rides his bicycle to the Tsukiji fish market each morning to buy the fish, octopus, shrimp, and eel to be served that day, he already knows who will have the very best of the best. Each supplier is an individual expert and Jiro has committed to long-term relationships with each. The tuna buyer selects the very best tuna available at Tsukiji each day, which he then proudly offers to Sukiyabashi Jiro.

Third, Jiro is driven to create for the delight of his customers. For years, Jiro directed his apprentices to massage the octopus for thirty minutes before it was ready to be served.

But in the spirit of continual improvement (*kaizen*) famously embraced by the Japanese automobile industry and other manufacturers after World War II, Jiro decided he could and should do better. So instead of thirty minutes of massage, Jiro's apprentices were directed to massage the octopus for forty to forty-five minutes prior to serving each day, to make it even more tender and flavorful.

Fourth, he and his team taste their creations, ensuring that each ingredient is at its peak of perfection. Everyone working in the restaurant is expected to take little nibbles of the ingredients throughout the day—a piece of fish here, a sliver of sea urchin there. If something doesn't taste quite right, then it is discarded and will never get anywhere near a customer's plate.

Fifth, and perhaps most important, Jiro is a *shokunin*—"a person who embodies the artisan spirit of the relentless pursuit of perfection through his craft."[3] Jiro is never satisfied with the status quo. He knows that his integrity is on the line each and every day, and that if something can be improved, he will do it—regardless of the cost or the extra time required. Nothing short of perfection is acceptable to Jiro, but he knows that perfection is a state of becoming. It is an ideal that is never reached but that must always be strived for and pursued.

Jiro Ono is a man who is driven to create and protect the integrity of his ideas. For him there is no question how he produces his craft—he is an inventor, a living model, a person who never compromises on excellence.

Leadership Archetype: The Inventor

Nothing is more difficult than to introduce
a new order, because the innovator has for
enemies all those who have done well under
the old conditions and lukewarm defenders
in those who may do well under the new.

—Niccolò Machiavelli

Inventors constantly search for the best way to improve processes and products and to perfect their craft. They are experimenters who make many small bets and are willing to fail in pursuit of big wins. They ask the question, **"How can we make this better?"**

For inventors, maintaining the integrity of their ideas is paramount. They are possessed with vision, and compromise is not an option. They make choices for what is best for the idea, and they execute with excellence. Inventors have high standards and challenge others to meet them. They may test you, they may challenge you, they may teach you, and sometimes they may insult you—but it is all in the interest of building a faithful team that will make their vision a reality. Their integrity motivates them to fight to protect every detail. By definition, an inventor is not satisfied by the status quo, but aspires for high standards and excellence each and every time.

The Key to the Inventor's Success: Integrity

> Achievement of your happiness is the only
> moral purpose of your life, and that happiness,
> not pain or mindless self-indulgence, is the
> proof of your moral integrity, since it is the
> proof and the result of your loyalty to the
> achievement of your values.
>
> —Ayn Rand

Former U.S. senator Alan K. Simpson once said, "If you have integrity, nothing else matters. If you don't have integrity, nothing else matters."[4]

In English, integrity means *firm adherence to a moral code*.

In Latin, it means *to be whole*—you bring *all* of who you are, good and bad, strengths and weaknesses, together.

In French, it means *intact*—you are able to stay intact with who you are under any circumstances, even if there are consequences.

In Hebrew, it means *force*. When you have integrity you are a force to be reckoned with.

When I refer to integrity, I have something very specific in mind:

Character. Identifying *who* you are and what is right and wrong for you. (*Who* you are.)

Convictions. Acknowledging your convictions to act accordingly. (*What* you are.)

Code of conduct. Honoring your personal code of conduct and *how* you will act. (*How* you are.)

To have integrity you have to know *who* you are; you have to know *what* you stand for; and you have to know *how* to act in honor of your code. This *who, what,* and *how* all add up to create a *whole* person—a person who is unified, undivided, and a remarkably powerful force in the world. When a person of high integrity invents, there is no stopping him.

A person of integrity is willing to bear the consequences of his innovations—whether it be disrupting a marketplace or changing lives. He follows his convictions no matter what obstacles stand in his way because a person of integrity stands for *all* of who he is, *all* of what he is, and *all* of how he is. The person who lives with integrity does what is right, not because he has to but because it is right for him.

A few years ago, I was asked to give a keynote to a group of college students who were studying entrepreneurship. The group wanted me to base my talk on how to lead companies that produce results and become successful.

When the day arrived, I stood at the front of the room and said, "I am here to speak to you about integrity." The students broke out in applause.

Their reaction gratified me. When I am asked to speak about producing results and becoming more successful, most people want me to speak about becoming faster and quicker in business, or lowering costs. But these ambitious students were not looking for shortcuts, quick fixes, or best practices on how to supercharge their success. They wanted meaningful insight and I came to give it to them.

I told them that no matter what career they pursued in their future, or what kind of leadership style they cultivated, or what innovation they developed, they would be held accountable and responsible as *people*. As I explained to the students, *everything* in business, leadership, and success is founded on the virtue of integrity—it's the force that leads the way.

Integrity is not a concept taught in business school, and it is not measured as an achievable goal or outcome in business plans. But without integrity, there is no innovation. There is no progress. There is no meaningful success.

No leader can foster advancement in business without trust, honesty, confidence, and respect. That in sum is integrity.

Integrity is cultivated by:

Honoring commitments. Be accountable and responsible for what you say and do.

Speaking with honesty. An uncomfortable truth may hurt for a little while, but a lie will hurt forever. Having integrity is speaking the *whole* truth, even when it may have a negative effect on the relationship.

Maintaining a consistent moral code. Doing what is right is not always easy, but those who have integrity do not compromise their moral code, even if it means there will be consequences.

Embracing unwavering convictions. Innovation demands commitment. Never compromise your vision.

Treating everyone with respect. The surest way to cultivate loyalty is to treat everyone with the same respect you'd expect. Even if it does not mean anything to you, it could just mean *everything* to them.

Establishing trust. Where there is no trust, there is no progress. Effective leaders inspire faith in their vision. Your team has to trust you before they will follow you.

When respect is earned, honesty appreciated, commitment valued, and trust gained, then integrity will surely grow. When they are not, integrity will find another home.

If people cannot trust your word—cannot understand your motivations, cannot respect your character—your ideas are worthless, because you will never build the team you need to make them a reality.

Integrity starts with *you*. Make it the heart and soul of your leadership and your business.

A lack of integrity is easy to detect. When words don't match actions, when actions don't match promises, and when commitments are not kept, a team cannot coalesce. Innovation cannot happen. Aspirations cannot be achieved.

In the end, I convinced the college students that to be a great leader, an innovator, an inventor, they must consistently act with integrity. To persuade people to follow your vision and manifest your ideas, you must be believable; to be believable you must be credible; and to be credible you must be honorable.

The Inventor's Leadership Gap: Corruption

Corruption is like a ball of snow, once it's set a rolling it must increase.
—Charles Caleb Colton

When George and James came together to start a design firm in a large metropolitan city, they had a great vision and great heart. They wanted to build a business that would be meaningful and have integrity in its work.

George was the artist in the partnership—he had attended a famous school of design in New England, and he guided the firm's creative decisions. James was an MBA who enjoyed working the nuts and bolts of the organization. He was the one who made sure customers paid their bills on time, and that their vendors and employees were kept happy. The two men worked hard, and it looked as though they were headed for great success. But two years after the company's launch, I got a call from George, who was clearly upset.

"I don't understand it," said George. "We built this business together from the ground up, and James is being so reckless! I just cannot imagine why he would do that."

What George didn't know was that James had been making plans to demolish the company for a long time. George thought they were creating something *together,* but James had other ideas—he was out for himself.

I knew this because James had called me a few months earlier to help *him.*

During my meeting with James, he told me he had concerns about George as a partner, and he wanted me to help him sort things out. When James and I spoke again, he hinted that he had some ethical concerns about George. He did not come out and say what these ethical issues might be—in fact, he was vague and evasive about the whole thing. This didn't feel right to me. I had known both of them when we worked together to start up their company, and it seemed to me that George being called unethical was out of line. Was James trying to cast suspicion on George's character? I knew there was more to this story than what James was telling me. I could see James was facing his leadership gap.

When people act in a way they know is unethical, they are corrupt. And they look for allies to make them feel right. After a few days, it was very clear to me what was happening—James was trying to enlist me as an ally. Moral corruption happens all the time in businesses, in teams, and in families. But I wasn't having it.

James was ready to move on with the business on his own, leaving his partner, George, behind. But instead of coming right out and saying what he wanted, he went about it corruptly. James worked to tarnish George's character by calling him unethical. He attempted to alienate his partner by enlisting allies to his side.

James thought he had my attention, and he did, but not in the way he had hoped. It was obvious to me that James was trying to paint a picture of George as unethical, uncaring, self-centered, domineering, and incompetent, but, in truth, everyone I spoke to at the company described *James* that way—not George. The roots of James's character were showing, and his trying to get me on his side demonstrated he lacked integrity.

Unfortunately, the seeds of the breakup of this partnership had been planted, and there was no going back. I helped them work out the dissolution of their business partnership so they could go their separate ways and form their own companies, which they did. George was, of course, devastated. He didn't know how he could run his own company without James by his side.

George kept saying to me, "I feel betrayed; I don't understand what happened. I wanted this to work—I worked very hard on our partnership. Why would he do this to me? Why would he betray me this way?"

As it turned out, James's corruption became George's blessing, and James's lack of character ended up costing him. When we separated the company, not one employee wanted to go with James, but everyone wanted to go with George. James's business ultimately failed, while George's thrived.

The person with integrity does the right thing even when no one else will, and even if no one else is looking—not because he thinks it will change the world, but because he refuses to be changed by the world. The person of integrity does not need to be a Mahatma Gandhi or a Mother Teresa, he only needs to have a grasp on values that can set high standards, help guide actions, and inspire others to follow his lead.

A true test of integrity isn't how you are on the best days, but how you act on the worst days. The inner attitude of your mind has the power to change the outer aspect of your life. Don't allow your mind to tell your heart what to do, because the mind gives in too easily while the heart fights for its convictions. When you understand what your convictions are, they enable you to leverage your strengths and manage your weaknesses. Integrity makes you whole. It allows you to be cognizant of the impact and force you have on others.

There are many different temptations that threaten to corrupt our integrity each and every day, and these temptations are well summarized by the seven deadly sins: wrath, greed, sloth, pride, lust, envy, and gluttony. In addition to these eternal sins, the strong but negative emotions we might feel from time to time are also enemies of integrity. These negative emotions corrupt integrity and destroy it: hubris without humility; rage without conscience; prejudice without tolerance; sacrifice without resentment; and shame without humanity. If we allow them to take over, they will wedge a gap between who we are and what we want to achieve.

The Inventor's Leadership Gap Archetype: The Destroyer

> If we destroy something around us we destroy ourselves.
>
> —Buddha

Corrupt leaders destroy their organizations from within, doing very real damage to their people, their customers, and their communities. Instead of rallying people to aspire to create advancements—better ideas, better products, better employees, better teams—they make things worse in the pursuit of their own goals. A leader without integrity is corrupt. A leader who is not inventing is a leader who is destroying.

The destroyer is not only corrupt with his business, but reckless with his people's minds, hearts, and lives.

Leveraging the Destroyer Within

First you destroy those who create values.
Then you destroy those who know what the
values are, and who also know that those
destroyed before were in fact the creators of
values. But real barbarism begins when no
one can any longer judge or know that what
he does is barbaric.

—Ryszard Kapuściński

An inventor has integrity, a destroyer is corrupt, and the gap between them is clear. These two opposing leadership styles are distinguished by actions. The destroyer's lack of integrity permits quick fixes, cutting corners, and compromising quality and standards. An inventor is committed to putting his personal values into practice rather than simply professing them. To overcome the leadership gap of the destroyer, you must unequivocally uphold high standards; allow integrity to be the guiding force of your ideas, your mission, and your leadership; and choose greatness over gallantry every time.

Consider your priorities: Does your idea serve the good of

many, or does it serve only yourself? If you intend to become a great leader, rethink on which side of the gap you stand, because the choice is yours in any given situation. You can be a creator of great things by holding fast to your convictions without compromise. But without that depth of integrity, you will find yourself trapped in the gap of the destroyer—corrupt, unscrupulous, and immoral.

Look for what is good, not what is bad. A destroyer tends to look at things in a negative way, canceling out the good. The only way to shift things around and to leverage the parts of your creativity, talent, and strengths is by cultivating a habit of looking at the positive. Positivity is a powerful tool that can be pulled out of your pocket whenever you feel vulnerable in a certain situation, or when you feel like something uncomfortable or distressing has happened. It's a master key needed to open life's doors that cannot be opened otherwise.

Instead of criticizing, try complimenting. The destroyer is always finding fault in how things are done and how things shouldn't be done. When you are constantly criticizing, you don't get more of what you want—you get less of what you need. Instead, try finding what is right with people instead of what is wrong, and watch them excel at what they do.

Be who you want to see in the world. People don't trust a destroyer. If you want people to trust you, be trustworthy. If you want people to respect you, be respectful. If you want loyalty, be loyal. Destroyers need to understand that they must become what they want to see in the world.

Avoid cutting corners. Every destroyer needs to understand that nothing great was ever accomplished by cutting corners or skimping on excellence. Never cut corners and never accept anything that is second-rate. Success is achieved by having integrity for a craft, a force for change, and, most of all, boldness to be honorable. Destroyers are only fooling themselves if they think they can get ahead by cutting corners.

Being a destroyer makes corrupt what is good, and makes what is great unattainable.

Becoming an Inventive Leader

We want to encourage a world of creators, of inventors, of contributors, because this world that we live in, this interactive world, is ours.

—Ayah Bdeir

Of all the principles of character, integrity might just be the most critical. The word *character* is derived from the Greek word *charassein,* which means to sharpen or engrave. This meaning itself provides us with a much richer understanding of what our character needs to be—sharply defined and clearly visible to others. It is not unattainable nor is it unachievable; it is something that can be developed and strengthened.

Shaping integrity requires a humble introspection into

who we are, and it seeks wisdom from our vast experience. Our character is constantly asking us to take a closer look at our deepest motivation.

Integrity can never be a self-righteous declaration of character, because integrity continuously asks us to be true to ourselves. It consistently asks us to be authentic to who we are and what we do, and in turn it tells us that in order to embrace integrity we must have it engraved into our character. We need to develop the ability to wrestle with the urges within ourselves—understanding our faults, identifying our weaknesses, and relating them to their consequences—because our character of integrity won't allow us to rationalize or compartmentalize our gaps.

Integrity is a personal choice that requires a consistent commitment to honor moral, ethical, spiritual, and artistic principles without compromise.

Integrity takes intellectual ownership that produces authenticity, transparency, and virtue. At all times, our actions must mirror our words in everything we do.

At all times, our words must mirror the expression of our intentions.

Integrity as a character can be engraved within us only when we are accountable to our ethical principles.

As the philosopher Albert Schweitzer once explained, "The tragedy of life is not that we die, but is rather, what dies inside a man while he lives." If we destroy the parts of who we are, we become corrupt; the forces of creativity and invention will die within us.

In Kabbalah, there are two sides of the tree of life. On

one side you have the choice of understanding wisdom, and on the other you have the structure to manage your choices.

Integrity is the sum of all our parts. A wholeness is derived from the wisdom of our choices and how we manage those choices.

The integrity to invent must be like breathing—something we do but rarely *think* about doing.

Become an inventor and transcend the destroyer's leadership gap step-by-step:

Get to know yourself. Integrity first starts with principles, intentions, and values. Integrity is ingrained behavior based on values rather than personal gain. Integrity alone won't make you a great leader, but without integrity you will never be one. Know yourself, and keep knowing yourself; rethink who you are at all times you are leading.

Set high personal standards. Inventors are driven to be the best they can be and judge themselves against a standard of excellence. Everything inventors produce must be original and beyond what others expect. Inventors will make an extra effort to stand out from the crowd. People keep their eyes on leaders and imitate the great ones—how they act, how they speak. If you seek greatness, bring the best parts of yourself and your ideas forward with the greatest force.

Honor commitments. Simply put: Do everything you say you are going to do. If for any reason you cannot keep your commitments or your promise, take responsibility. Be accountable. Be reliable. Be decisive. And be unwavering.

Value truthful communication. Most leaders prefer to communicate good news and avoid communicating bad news. But effective communication is honest, clear, and concise. It's not distance that keeps people apart, but a lack of communication. Assumptions are not only the number one relationship killer, they undermine leadership, too.

Make conscious choices. Doing the right thing isn't always easy, especially when shortcuts beckon. But minding your leadership gaps means rethinking how you do things and why you do them. Exercise wisdom. Integrity is always the right way.

Treat others with respect. Integrity demands respect, and inventors are vigilant about being courteous and considerate. Be respectful toward cultural differences, political positions, creative opinions, and all distinctions in race, age, and sexual orientation. Inventors value original thinking and expression— and they show respect for those who exercise it.

Strive for excellence. If you don't want to fall into a habit of corrupt, destructive practices, make striving for excellence a habit. Excellence can be doing ordinary things extraordinarily well; and most of the time, if not all the time, excellence is not a skill but an attitude.

GREAT INVENTOR LEADERS

Walt Disney, whose integrity was so great that he insisted the eyes of the wicked stepsisters in the mural of

Cinderella in Disneyland's Magic Kingdom castle be painted twelve times with different shades of green, before he found the one that best communicated his idea of envy.

Lin-Manuel Miranda, who pushed boundaries in his creative interpretation of history in the musical *Hamilton* (particularly through his diverse-casting practices), but still maintained the integrity of the play's historical details diligently, faithfully, and without compromise.

Blake Mycoskie, the founder and Chief Shoe Giver of TOMS, and the person behind the idea of One for One, a business model that helps a person in need with every product purchased. Blake invents things that people need, and he does it with the highest standards and integrity.

Inventors embody a special breed of leadership centered on innovating with excellence. The ones who achieve greatness have unwavering integrity and refuse to compromise. Think of Jiro, who set a new standard for sushi throughout the world and whose integrity inspired loyalty in those who did business with him. Inventors are not just those who relentlessly pursue excellence. They are those who define it.

Recognizing Yourself in the Inventor Archetype

The inventor maintains his or her integrity while thinking outside the box.

THE INVENTOR

Are you an inventor? Ask yourself these questions:

- Why is having a higher standard important to you?

- What inspires you to be creative?

- What blocks your creativity and creative flow?

- In what ways does your recklessness cause problems for you?

- Do you do what is expected of you, or do you do what is right? Why?

CHAPTER SEVEN

THE NAVIGATOR

The navigator is a trusted leader who steers people
toward pragmatic workable outcomes, uncomplicated
solutions, and powerful results.

Ester Fuchs is an esteemed professor of public affairs and
political science, and director of the Urban and Social
Policy Program at Columbia University's School of International and Public Affairs. From 2002 to 2005, Ester served as
New York City mayor Michael Bloomberg's special adviser
for governance and strategic planning. She was put in charge
of three key mayoral initiatives, and she was the first woman
to serve as chair of the New York City Charter Revision
Commission.

But her beginnings were much humbler.

Ester was raised in an Orthodox Jewish home in Bayside,
Queens, the third of five children. Her mother was active in
the community, and her father—a Polish immigrant—was a

diamond cutter who served in his synagogue as cantor for forty years. From an early age, Ester was attuned to the world around her, and she became politically active. According to Ester, her first political memory was of the 1963 assassination of President John F. Kennedy. The quote next to Ester's photo in her eighth-grade yearbook was "It's not fair."

She graduated from Bayside High School when she was just sixteen, and then attended Queens College. During that time, Ester was elected to the county committee, and she took part in an anti–Vietnam War demonstration that shut down the Long Island Expressway. She earned a master's degree from Brown University and a PhD from the University of Chicago, and eventually returned to New York to teach, first at Barnard and then at Columbia.

Ester Fuchs accomplished something few people are able to do successfully: she navigated and bridged the traditional gap between the ivory towers of academia and the gritty reality of street politics in America's most populous and diverse city. Ester has the rare ability to address some of the city's most challenging problems by searching for and finding new solutions, and then bringing the right people to the table to implement them. She accomplishes this by trusting others—and earning their trust in return.

Making the move from academia to governing New York City wasn't easy for Ester Fuchs, but within nine months, she figured out how to navigate City Hall and apply her problem-solving approach to the government sausage grinder. As Ester puts it, "All the things that I thought were great advantages actually turned out to be great disadvantages. I thought, okay,

I'm willing to work hard and I want to get stuff done and I don't owe anybody anything. It turned out that all of those qualities were very unappealing to people who were in government because how could you control that person? How do you manage somebody like that?"[1]

Ester realized that she could make her mark by identifying, planning, and implementing her own projects on behalf of Mayor Bloomberg, whose complete trust in her resulted in Ester being dubbed "the left hemisphere" of the mayor's brain by one newspaper reporter.[2]

While Ester cares passionately about the issues that confront her fellow New Yorkers on a daily basis, she also cares about preparing and navigating the next generation of young minds for their role in dealing with these problems. Ester says, "Most people are not informed, so I teach my class to *rethink* problems. Students have to understand the dynamic of how you understand the problem and how you deal with the political process to ensure that change actually takes place. It's not enough to have the objective solution to problems if you don't understand the relationships between the state and city governments, how interest-group politics works, how to use the political process to enact change, and how to navigate the political process."[3]

One of the problems that Ester tackled with her students was the issue of large amounts of trash being thrown into Jamaica Bay in Queens.

As Ester explained to her students, the easiest option would be to simply pick up the phone and call your counterpart in the Sanitation Department. You could ask that person to arrange to put more trash cans on the shore of Jamaica Bay, or step up collection efforts. This approach, however, might cause consequences you didn't anticipate, such as the need to increase the city budget for this neighborhood, or deal with homeless people who rummage through the trash cans. And it doesn't really get to the root of the problem, which is people throwing trash into Jamaica Bay.

Alternatively, you could try to figure out who it is that's putting the garbage in Jamaica Bay. That seems like a simple, obvious thing—something you might not even bother thinking about. This requires digging deeper to try to understand why there's so much of a particular type of garbage in Jamaica Bay, versus another body of water, like the Hudson River on Manhattan's west side. As it turns out, when you navigate deeper, you'll find there is a large Hindu community in Queens, and some of them perform their religious practices at the bay. The garbage is primarily food and wrappers that are introduced into the bay as offerings.[4]

So the solution then becomes something related to the polluters—who are these people? They don't understand that their ritual practice has consequences. The best approach in this case might be to meet with the leaders of the religious community to try to explain to them what is happening in the bay, and ask them to come up with a way to perform their religious practices that doesn't leave trash and food debris in the water. Performing this line of thinking led Ester to an efficient and effective solution.

Mayor Bloomberg trusted her and relied on her to be his eyes and ears on the ground. She had held no political office before—but she possessed not only a smart mind but a smart navigator's heart.

At Columbia, Ester's students trust her because she helps them navigate and solve complex and thorny issues in practical and pragmatic ways.

Ester Fuchs is a navigator who leads others to smarter solutions—whether they are her students, or those in government or in her community.

Ester Fuchs is no ordinary woman. She accomplishes extraordinary feats with the heart of the navigator, in practical, pragmatic ways. You might think this is a quality that is found in everyone, but think again. Many of us look at problems and seek solutions, but we don't necessarily get results. The gift and the extraordinary talent of Ester Fuchs is that she's willing to rethink everything she knows to understand problems in fresh ways, and get right to the heart of the matter. While most people would be lost in the details, what makes Ester Fuchs remarkable, and what most of us take for granted, is that she navigates through difficult situations with a firm and reassuring mind that inspires trust.

You cannot navigate people if they don't trust you. You cannot spark change in an organization if no one follows. The navigator takes you to new places, and you trust her enough to follow. The navigator encourages you to take new approaches to problems and to come up with better solutions that get results. This is why Ester Fuchs is the trusted adviser to some of the most important people of our time and generation.

Leadership Archetype: The Navigator

A mind that is stretched to a new idea,
never returns to its original dimension.
—Oliver Wendell Holmes

Navigators know where they need to go and they take people there. And they do this with such credence that people trust and follow them. Navigators have a way of making the complicated simple, and the simple understandable. They masterfully steer their organization and the people within it to even better outcomes. But first, navigators must be able to navigate *themselves*.

Navigators ask the question, **"How can we get to where we need to go?"**

The Key to the Navigator's Success: Trust

Building trust begins with an appreciation
and understanding of trust, but it also
requires practice and practices.
—Robert C. Solomon

Trust is inherent in a navigator. First, they trust themselves and their own ability to lead. But in order for a navigator to succeed, he must build *his trust* in others even as he earns their trust in return. A navigator has the unique responsibility to understand trust, earn trust, and build trust all at the same time.

Trust begins from within. It begins by acknowledging your own worth—it's a validation of self.

When a leader trusts himself, he knows how to trust his followers.

When a boss knows how to trust himself, he knows how to trust his employees.

When teachers know how to trust themselves, they know how to trust their students.

When students don't trust themselves, they usually don't trust authority.

When parents know how to trust themselves, they know how to trust their children.

All trust begins from within.

We must learn to value ourselves.

We must learn to honor ourselves.

Trust is defined in the dictionary as a "firm belief in the reliability, truth, ability, or strength of someone or something."[5] For many years I used that definition when speaking to leaders and organizations about trust, but when I explored further, I found that the word *trust* in Hebrew is *batach* (written as בָּטַח).

In addition to "trust," *batach* means to feel safe, and to be careless.

To be *careless*?

The word caught my eye because careless is the antithesis of trust, right?

And again I had to ask myself, what does *careless* mean as it relates to trust?

After much thought, I understood. When you trust someone, you don't have to worry that he will attack you, or take advantage of you, or try to tear you down. You can engage in the relationship without a care, knowing that you are safe. Being without a care is a privilege that gives us a remarkable sense of freedom and fulfillment. Trust is access to another person without worry; it allows us to be carefree; it allows us to feel safe; it allows us freedom; and it allows us to be who we really are—without pretense or concern.

But trust opens us up to the possibility of being hurt.

So why do we take that risk? The underlying truth is that we achieve so much more by working together than by working alone.

Whether we are a head of state, CEO, leader, worker, volunteer, student, parent, teacher, or anyone else, most situations we experience during the course of an average day involve some amount of trust. And the amount of trust you are willing to build with others can help you move forward in your life and career—or it can hold you back.

In my practice, I regularly encounter people who don't trust themselves and have a hard time trusting others.

The science of trust is today mostly built on the research of the hormone oxytocin, which has a powerful effect on human emotions and actions. In the science journal *Nature,* the researchers Michael Kosfeld, Markus Heinrichs, Paul Zak, Urs Fischbacher, and Ernst Fehr state,

> Here we show that intranasal administration of oxytocin, a neuropeptide that plays a key role in social attachment and affiliation in non-human mammals, causes a substantial increase in trust among humans, thereby greatly increasing the benefits from social interactions.[6]

This line of research began in 2001 when Paul Zak conducted trust experiments on college students, based on his belief that oxytocin would change the way they interacted with people they had never met—perfect strangers. Zak and his fellow researchers recruited a group of students for the experiment, then gave each participant $10 just for showing up. In a TED talk, Zak explained how the experiment went from there:

> Then we match them in pairs by computer. And in that pair, one person gets a message saying, "Do you want to give up some of your $10 you earned for being here and ship it to someone else in the lab?" The trick is you can't see them; you can't talk to them. You only do it one time. Now whatever you give up gets tripled in the other person's account. You're going to make them a lot wealthier. And they get a message by computer saying person one sent you this

amount of money. Do you want to keep it all, or do you want to send some amount back?[7]

According to Zak, the initial transfer of cash from the first person to the second is a measure of trust. The second transfer of cash—from the second person back to the first—is a measure of trustworthiness. Zak says, ". . . economists were flummoxed on why the second person would ever return any money. They assumed money is good; why not keep it all?"

But that's not what happened. Ninety percent of the students who were in the first-decision position sent money to the other party. Most surprising to the researchers, 95 percent of the students who had received money—who were in the second-decision position—returned some of the money to the student who had given it to them in the first place. According to Zak,

> by measuring oxytocin we found that the more money the second person received, the more their brain produced oxytocin, and the more oxytocin on board, the more money they returned. So we have a biology of trustworthiness.[8]

When you do something nice for someone else, their brains will give them the push they need to drop their defenses and to respond in kind. This is the powerful biochemical basis of trust, and it is something we can build more of with those in our businesses and in our lives. The more oxytocin our brains produce, the more we trust, and the happier we are.

The way we treat ourselves sets the standard for how we treat others.

The way others treat us is the way we will treat ourselves. Don't settle for anything other than trust.

The Navigator's Leadership Gap: Arrogance

> The smaller the mind the greater the conceit.
>
> —Aesop

My client is the subject of numerous business newspaper and magazine articles—a very accomplished executive. Despite his high profile in the media, in his industry, and in the business community, his leadership lacked engagement. The company's HR director called me in with the hope that I would be able to help this CEO implement a new change initiative within their organization. I was given a very short and direct challenge: "Help us get people to buy in to it."

I met with the CEO in his mahogany-paneled office suite at the company's headquarters—located in a tall skyscraper in one of the nation's largest cities. To get the ball rolling during our first meeting, I asked the CEO to provide me with some background about the coming change initiative. He responded with lots of talk about change, and why change is important. He seemed to be very well prepared on the need for change, which was great, but then I started to ask more-detailed, clarifying questions, such as: How did they plan to roll out the change initiative? How were they going to have their people buy in to the change?

The CEO shot back with such arrogance in his voice, it stunned me. "We will tell them what to do and they will do it."

"Is that actually your plan?" I asked him.

"Yes," the CEO replied.

I told him that change initiatives are a little bit more complicated than just telling people what to do.

He looked at me and said, "Isn't it your job as a consultant to make sure that the rollout is successful?"

"What about the people?" I asked. "Are you going to take them into consideration?"

"We will just tell them what they have to do, and they will have to do it," he repeated.

"And what about you?" I asked. "Will you be doing your part?"

"What do you mean?" he asked, by now more than a bit peeved with my line of questioning.

"Well, nothing changes until you do," I explained.

The CEO nodded his head like he understood, but I could tell he did not actually understand the importance of my question. It was evident that his idea about implementing a change initiative was to trust that whatever he ordered to do would happen.

But I was frank with him and told him that this is not how things work—and that his change initiative would not only fail; it would be an *epic* failure.

And then I told him something else he did not want to hear: "You have to be part of the initiative to make it successful. It has to come from you, and it has to start with you."

He said, "I am too busy for all of this. I just want you to make it happen—this is why we hired you!"

"If *you* are too busy to make it happen," I asked, "don't you think everyone else feels the same way, too? They will also be too busy to make it happen. If you don't make the time, how do you expect anyone else to make the time?"

It took a while to get the CEO to understand that he would have to take responsibility. The first thing I had to do was make sure he understood that if any change were going to happen, it would first have to start with him. The change would then ripple out into the organization, the culture, and his people.

In his mind, as a leader, he commands people and they embrace his ideas. But his leadership gap was his arrogance. This CEO expected his people to simply trust whatever he said and do it. Bossing people around was his idea of leadership.

I left the CEO with a very important message: "You get trust when you give trust." When you trust your people, when you give them what they need, when you make them part of the vision, they will trust you in return. Trust them, and they will follow your lead. Not the other way around.

The Navigator's Leadership Gap Archetype: The Fixer

Suffering attracts fixers the way road-kills attract vultures.

—Eugene H. Peterson

When we want to navigate for others, sometimes we go too far, and we step on people's toes. Hence, the navigator's leadership gap is the fixer: wanting to help too much, fix too much, and rescue too much.

The leadership gap between the navigator and the fixer is a very fine line that is sometimes difficult to recognize. For a navigator to effectively lead a team to a new destination, a new idea, a new venture, or a new solution, he must have earned the utmost trust of his people. On the other hand, if a leader is conceited or demanding, expecting that others simply follow, that leader inspires no one to do so. No one likes a know-it-all.

The fixer is a navigator no one trusts.

These are the most common ways navigators violate boundaries to become fixers:

When the navigator becomes a chronic rescuer. When you are the uninvited helper who cannot resist the temptation to jump in and fix *every* single problem, it soon becomes an annoyance to those you're trying to help. While the intention may be good, the attention is just too much. The chronic rescuer has a life of his own, but his hopes and goals are tied up with those of others. Fixers see the needs of others as more important than their own, and they move from *wanting* to help to *needing* to help. They want other people to need them, and will go from one person to the next—offering assistance along the way—to gain a sense of being needed.

When the navigator becomes a long-standing fixer. When you go from solving problems to having a deep desire to *save* people, it's easy to see how this can cause a lot of trouble. These well-meaning navigators often pursue careers in the helping professions in which they can control and fix other people. They think they know best about what works and what does not work for others, and they exhaust themselves trying to take care of everyone else. However, perhaps even worse, they feel utterly rejected when their assistance is no longer necessary or welcomed.

When the navigator becomes an emotional caretaker. When you start self-sacrificing, then you know that you are not a navigator anymore. Instead, you have become an emotionally dependent person who *insists* on helping. It's not so much about guiding or steering, but about getting so absorbed by other people's problems that this is used as a way of escaping the responsibility of taking care of oneself.

When the navigator becomes the sacrificial victim. Sometimes navigators take on the role of martyr. By constantly putting the needs of others before their own needs, they get a sense that they are needed. Self-sacrificing for the needs of others is never a good thing. These people often neglect themselves due to a neurotic obsession to look after others. They are never really content because they don't pay attention to their own needs and they constantly feel burned-out. Even so, they will persist in helping even when it has been made clear by others that their help is not needed.

When the navigator becomes a micromanager. If you are never satisfied with how people do things, then you are a micromanager. If how others work always frustrates you, then you are a micromanager. If you think you are the only one who can get things done—and done the right way—you are a micromanager. In each of these examples, you are doing more damage to your organization and the people within it than good.

Have you crossed the boundary?

- Do you find yourself helping others without them asking you for help?

- Do you insist on helping others in the way *you* believe they need to be helped, instead of how *they* believe they need to be helped?

- Do you hope your rescuing actions will get others to admire you?

- Do you struggle to focus on or complete your own work because you are too drained from running errands for others?

- Do you feel totally powerless and worthless when you cannot help someone?

- Do you help others primarily because it feels like the best way for you to gain positive attention?

If you answered yes to one or more of these questions, then you have a problem with boundaries. And depending on how big it is, this problem will interfere with your ability to be a successful navigator.

If you can see elements of the fixer in your leadership style, trust is the leadership gap that stands between you and your greatness. Spend some time rethinking what you know about trust and how it can make or break your leadership. After all, being a great leader means being able to be the one others trust to steer the organization in pursuit of a vision.

The navigator is very much the twin to the explorer—the explorer seeks new land, while the navigator steers the boat to the shore to investigate.

The navigator helps us rethink what we know.

To rethink what we don't even know we don't know.

The navigator is the one who ignites us . . .

To learn something new.

To hear something unique.

To see something different.

The navigator knows how to touch our hearts, because trust is in place.

Leveraging the Fixer Within

> *Deciding what not to do is as important as deciding what to do.*
>
> —Steve Jobs

Navigators run into trouble when they don't respect boundaries. For every good navigator who has discovered what he is looking for, there is a navigator who has lost his way in the leadership gap. Here are some ways to leverage the fixer within:

Learn to fix the fixer. Before you fix anyone, you have to fix yourself. Hire a great coach or get a supportive friend to help heal the wounds you were given as a child and deal with all the loss you've experienced as an adult. This may be the hardest part of leveraging the fixer within you—it's much easier said than done, because as human beings we are complicated, and as fixers we want to simplify everything.

Trust people to fend for themselves. By helping others, you don't allow them to fend for themselves. Instead of always offering to rescue, nurse, comfort, defend, or support, learn to be a better listener and a more understanding person. Be compassionate and considerate, but don't offer to take over and take care of a situation that is concerning another person. Learn just to be there for someone else.

Be mindful of boundaries. If you are a fixer, you sometimes can get swallowed up in other people's challenges and problems and in turn lose sight of your own boundaries. If this sounds familiar to you, you can reduce this by minding your boundaries and shielding yourself from *emotional hostage syndrome,* which I have coined with my clients. This is when you feel things for another so strongly that you become a hostage of their emotions. When this happens you tend to lose yourself and do things you normally wouldn't do. If you get so caught up in other people's feelings that you lose sight of your own, establish a healthy boundary. Practice detachment from emotions of guilt and shame that can arise from the empathy that you may feel for the other, which may be leading you to do things you do not wish to do, and ultimately making you feel uncomfortable. In resisting this urge, you place responsibility for the other on them instead of on you, which is where it belongs in the first place.

Know they will still love you. If you are a fixer, you have a deep, strong need to be loved or liked, and because that is true, you are extremely careful not to do anything that would cause people around you to reject or abandon you. To cover up this side of you, you tend to fix and take care of things to gain the love of others. It's a hard truth to accept, but people don't need you to fix things for them to love you or stick around. Don't allow your fixing to become a relentless string of sacrifices. It never works being the martyr—no one ever wins.

The moment you stop being a fixer is the moment you understand the gift of navigating.

Becoming a Navigating Leader

> If your actions inspire others to dream
> more, learn more, do more, and become
> more, you are a leader.
>
> —John Quincy Adams

The last thing you might think about when it comes to classical music is the orchestra conductor as a navigator. For hundreds of years, conductors have pushed their own singular vision of musical scores on the musicians who serve in their orchestras—sometimes ruthlessly. Charles Hazlewood is a British conductor who leads orchestras all around the world. He is convinced that his job depends not on coercing the musicians in his orchestra, but on building their trust.

In his TED talk, Hazlewood says,

> In the old days, conducting, music making, was less about trust and more, frankly, about coercion. Up to and around the Second World War, conductors were invariably dictators—these tyrannical figures who would rehearse, not just the orchestra as a whole, but individuals within it, within an inch of their lives.[9]

However, with conductors like Charles Hazlewood taking the lead, this paradigm has been stood on its head. Hazlewood continues,

> We now have a more democratic view and way of making music—a two-way street. I, as the conductor, have to come to the rehearsal with a cast-iron sense of the outer architecture of that music, within which there is then immense personal freedom for the members of the orchestra to shine.[10]

To be an effective navigator and orchestra conductor, Hazlewood has to completely trust his mind, his ideas, and his body language. Because in every moment, and with every move, his facial expressions, words, and gestures have very definite outcomes.

He waves his baton and the orchestra plays.

He stops waving his baton and the orchestra stops.

In order for the members of the orchestra to listen and to understand and to act, they must trust their conductor's every move and gesture completely.

And Hazlewood also has to be in the position where he completely trusts the members of the orchestra to deliver the musical product that he envisions and hears within his head. Hazlewood says, "There has to be, between me and orchestra, an unshakeable bond of trust, born out of mutual respect, through which we can spin a musical narrative that we all believe in."[11]

For a conductor to be successful, he has to trust that he is speaking a language that the orchestra can understand. And the orchestra has to understand and trust what the conductor wants, and then deliver his gestures and signals as one body, everyone together. Trust is the way a beautiful piece of music comes together. And without it, everything breaks down.

When we understand each other, we trust each other.

When we trust each other, we make the most beautiful music together.

How does one build bridges of trust with another? By *paying attention* to communication, commitment, competence, and character.

Pay attention to: Communication. What's important is *how* people communicate—do they listen intently, or do they talk over others? Do they respond or do they react? How they communicate will determine whether or not we respect them.

Pay attention to: Commitment. What's important is whether or not people keep their commitments. Their level of commitment will determine how we respond to them.

Pay attention to: Competence. What's important is that people know what they are good at, and how their skills can contribute to making a difference. It is in competence that change will happen.

Pay attention to: Character. What's important is your character. Who you are and how you act are where trust will be given, earned, and cultivated.

Trust is the virtue that enforces the Golden Rule—when we treat others the way we would like to be treated, it makes the world a more moral place.

Trust is not just within us, it extends outward to those you know and to those you don't know—to your parents, colleagues, coworkers, peers, teachers, bosses, and leaders, and to the world. Having trusting interpersonal relationships is vital.

The greatest leaders are trustworthy and they create a culture of trust. According to the Great Place to Work Institute, which with *Fortune* magazine annually names the one hundred best companies to work for, committed and engaged employees who trust their management perform 20 percent better and are 87 percent less likely to leave their organizations. Not only that, but the financial performances of publicly traded companies on the "100 Best Companies to Work For" list outperform major stock indices by 300 percent, with half the voluntary turnover rates of their competitors.[12] Two-thirds of a company's survey score determining its ranking on the 100 Best Companies list is based on the results of the "Trust Index Employee Survey."

Trustworthy leaders lead fiscally sound companies. They are able to weather economic storms while their contemporaries struggle; they attract and keep their best talent; and they continue to innovate and solve problems at a high level.

They are master navigators who know how to guide, direct, encourage, and challenge their people to contribute their very best, because they ask the same of themselves as leaders.

Trustworthy leaders know that their relationships with others are key to their success, however success is measured for them.

Trustworthy leaders are also independent-minded enough to think for themselves and not just follow the pack. They are strong leaders who are mindful of what they want. They have a particular leadership style—the navigator—and know that it takes a group of people to come together to do something great. And the way to create something great starts with trust.

Demonstrate trust by honoring. Honor is given; it is bestowed. When you are honorable, it means you live your life by a certain code of conduct—one that is virtuous and moral. People show honor to those who trust honorable individuals.

Demonstrate trust by admiration. Showing admiration for people who are competent in skill and virtue—admiring them for who they are because it is something that pleases us or resonates for us. When we show admiration, we are saying, "I respect the way you make me feel" or "I respect the work that you do."

Demonstrate trust by appreciation. By showing appreciation, we recognize the accomplishment of a job well done. People might work for money, but they go the extra mile for recognition and admiration.

Demonstrate trust by esteem. When you hold someone in a high esteem, you are clearly demonstrating that you value him. If you have low esteem for someone, you don't value him as much.

Demonstrate by reverence. Showing others reverence comes from a profound feeling—a deep respect for another. Reverence is given to those whose virtues you hold in high regard.

In anything new, it is impossible to foresee everything that will come, but that is where the navigator excels. Navigators are good at overseeing, steering, guiding, and taking action—and self-correcting their path when necessary along the way.

They think a great deal and then they enlist the help of others.

They take into consideration talent and training and their responsibility of being the navigator—sometimes even maybe the teacher—and they learn to remain calm and to analyze each step of the way, because everything matters to the navigator.

Navigators establish themselves as people you can rely on because they . . .

Trust. Navigators show you the way by taking you along with them. They give and receive trust.

Are optimistic. Navigators have hope and confidence that what needs to get done will get done. They bring everything they have to the table—and more.

Love. Navigators know that love conquers all. They bring an unselfishness of heart and a taste for devotion. When people are deeply devoted to a cause, anything can happen.

GREAT NAVIGATOR LEADERS

Michael Bloomberg grew his business based on trusted information, then leveraged the trusted name he made for himself to lead NYC through a difficult financial crisis.

Sheryl Sandberg built a career on being a trusted adviser—first to Larry Summers, then to Mark Zuckerberg, and now to millions of women everywhere.

Nassim Nicholas Taleb focuses on problems of randomness, probability, and uncertainty, and he has a unique and powerful way of navigating problems that helps us find solutions.

Embrace the navigator archetype when you want to make a difference in your own life and in the lives of others. Boost your own leadership from good to great. If there are obstacles in the way, be the navigator who finds a pragmatic way around them. Constantly seek alternative paths with the determination to face challenges, while inviting others to join. Become the trusted navigator who steers instead of states, guides instead of manipulates, and pilots instead of controls.

Recognizing Yourself in the Navigator Archetype

The navigator knows the importance of trust. He provides pragmatic solutions rooted in rich experiences and grand perspectives. Are you a navigator? Ask yourself these questions:

- Who comes to you for counsel, and why?

- In what ways do you give advice when it has not been asked for?

- Do people come to you when they have problems? Why do you think that is the case?

- What do you do to see things in the bigger picture?

- If a task appears to be difficult or complex, do you naturally try to avoid it or tackle it, and what are the results?

CHAPTER EIGHT

THE KNIGHT

The knight is a loyal protector, champion, and defender with unwavering beliefs.

Did you know that the box of sugar-loaded cereal on your grocery store shelf, or the little tub of fat-free chocolate pudding in the refrigerated case (also chock-full of sugar), or those low-fat toaster pastries (once again, slathered with sugar) are healthy for you, but almonds, avocados, and salmon are not?

According to the politicians and bureaucrats who run the U.S. Food and Drug Administration (FDA), the answer is *yes.* In fact, the FDA decreed that processed snacks are healthier for Americans than unprocessed whole foods such as almonds, avocados, and salmon.

This strange but true story begins in 1990, when Congress passed the Nutrition Labeling Education Act, requiring the FDA to regulate the use of nutrient-content claims in food labeling. While the intent of the legislation was to ensure that unscrupulous food manufacturers didn't try to pass off unhealthy food as healthy, the Law of Unintended Consequences led to a variety of unexpected outcomes. In 1993, when the FDA defined the word *healthy,* the common consensus was that *any* sort of fat was considered bad, while carbohydrates (including sugar) were considered to be good. So to be considered healthy by the FDA, food had to be low in fat, or to have no fat at all.

Fast forward to March 17, 2015. The FDA issues an urgent warning letter to Daniel Lubetzky, founder and CEO of KIND, LLC, notifying his company that four of its popular snack bars were in violation of the Federal Food, Drug, and Cosmetic Act. Specifically, four of the KIND bars contain more than 1 gram of saturated fat, and more than 3 grams of total fat per 40 grams of product weight.

Even though the bars are relatively low in sugar, the nuts—almonds, cashews, peanuts—contained in the bars have natural fats. Therefore, according to the logic of the FDA, the bars are not worthy of being labeled good for you. In effect, KIND bars are unhealthy according to the letter of the law, even though the natural fats they contain are actually good for you.

Although these same nuts are currently recommended by the federal government as part of a healthy diet, the labeling rules have not yet been updated to reflect the current thinking. In fact, these guidelines still encourage the consumption of sugar and other carbs that were in vogue twenty years ago.

Daniel Lubetzky was morally offended by the FDA notice, and not just because the government letter could inspire the kind of bad press that gives chief marketing officers nightmares. Daniel had built an ethical company, and he is 100 percent loyal to the ideals that his company represents—to the customers who buy his products and to the communities in which they live. At the heart of everything Daniel does is this simple belief: There's more to business than profit. Daniel built KIND to make a positive difference in the world, and he is committed to doing whatever it takes to ensure that KIND improves people's lives without compromise.

By his eighth birthday, Daniel Lubetzky was already a quintessential entrepreneur. He had started his first business—conducting magic shows as a child in Mexico City. He moved to the United States with his family when he was a teenager, starting a lawn-mowing service and then a business selling watches at local flea markets. After he graduated from high school, Daniel enrolled in Trinity University, where he earned a BA (in economics and international relations), while expanding his watch business—renting kiosks from which to sell his products.

At Trinity, Daniel became interested in the ongoing Arab-Israeli conflict and began to wonder what he could do to help solve the region's problems. When Daniel was young, his father—a survivor of the Holocaust—told him stories about his experiences as a child during the Nazi occupation and in the concentration camps. Some of the stories were chilling and others inspiring. At Dachau, a Nazi guard felt pity for Daniel's starving father—and gave him a rotten potato to eat. If this act had been discovered by the camp's commander, the guard would have been severely punished. This small kindness—plus the tenacity to live—helped Daniel's father to survive.

After graduating from Stanford Law School and doing a short stint at McKinsey & Company, Daniel decided to put a promising legal career aside to accept a year-long fellowship in Israel. There he would help draft legislation based on a proposal for Arab-Israeli cooperation. In 1994, he started PeaceWorks, an organization devoted to "peace through enterprise" by marketing a popular line of pesto and tapenade produced by Israelis and Arabs, working together. Lubetzky says, "My efforts to build bridges among people can be directly drawn to my commitment to prevent what happened to my dad from happening again to others."[1]

After his father died in 2003, Daniel committed to honor his legacy through *kindness*—launching KIND in 2004 to create and sell healthy snack bars while building bridges between people. A little over a decade later, Daniel's company has sold more than one billion KIND bars, and also launched the KIND Movement, which according to the company has inspired more than one million acts of kindness—even as small as handing out cold drinks to construction workers, leading coat drives, writing thank-you notes to local heroes, and surprising coworkers with coffee. "The KIND Movement," says Lubetzky, "is a community where people connect emotionally to us because of what we are doing to drive change in the world."[2]

Daniel prides himself on being extremely loyal to his people and to the KIND cause. This loyalty is imbedded deep within every process and practice of the company, and it starts in the company's hiring process. Daniel says, "We are very particular about hiring because every full-time member of our team—which we refer to as family—will literally become a co-owner and shareholder who serves as an ambassador of the brand in their daily lives."[3]

Ultimately, the letter from the FDA didn't undo the KIND organization; it bolstered it. Make no mistake about it—there *was* negative publicity surrounding the FDA letter, but Daniel took the time to rethink what it meant to be an ethical company committed to its customers. KIND quickly announced that, with the support of "some of the world's foremost experts in nutrition, public health, and public policy," the company had filed a citizen petition with the FDA urging the agency to update its regulations around the term *healthy* in food labeling.[4]

Lubetzky says, "The experience was painful, but it made us stronger. When we look back five years from now, KIND will be leaping forward in health and wellness because of what we learned, and because of the loyal relationship we have with our customers."[5]

In May 2016, the FDA announced that it had reversed its decision and KIND could put "healthy" back on its label. The FDA also acknowledged (thanks in part to KIND's citizen petition) that the definition of "healthy" was in need of an update, and that the organization would seek input from the public and food experts.[6]

Even before the FDA took this action, Lubetzky was convinced he was doing the right thing. "In my mind," he says, "success is about remaining loyal to what you believe in. It is remaining loyal to an idea—it is remaining loyal to the people. If you want to do right by people, if you want to protect and champion a meaningful cause, you have to stay the course. If you want to do right by the world, you have to stay loyal to your vision—even if it gets difficult."[7]

Daniel Lubetzky is a *knight*—he is not only fiercely loyal to his people and his customers, but he is also loyal to his dream of having a positive impact on the world around him. He's not afraid to rethink what he knows and fight for what is right. Daniel says, "What I find most exciting about KIND—what makes me not want to sell the company—is the ability to prove to people that there is a new way of doing business. That you can put kindness at the forefront of what you do and serve those around you."[8]

With the loyalty and drive to serve that Daniel has dedicated to his company, team members, and customers, he has become an example of what happens when an irresistible force meets an immovable object. In Daniel's case, the object moves—and the world gets a little kinder. One snack and act at a time.

Leadership Archetype: The Knight

Fight on, brave knights! Man dies, but glory
lives! Fight on; death is better than defeat!
Fight on brave knights! for bright eyes
behold your deeds!

—Walter Scott

Knights are primarily associated with chivalry and protection, but they are driven by going to battle to defend their beliefs and are devoted to serve. Knights display fierce loyalty and partnership with others while protecting people and bonding them together. It is the knight who knows that leadership must have loyalty—the kind that is reliable and dependable and is filled with dedication. Knights will stand beside you and will serve you, before they serve themselves.

Knights are always asking, **"How can I serve *you*?"** while others are thinking, "How can I serve *me*?"

Shakespeare gave us a vision of the faithful knight when he wrote, "I will follow thee, to the last gasp, with truth and loyalty." Roman playwright Terence called the knight "a man of ancient virtue."

We are fortunate to find leaders who are loyal, and as leaders, we will be lucky to find people who are willing to stand by us through good times and bad. Loyalty is an essential element in both our professional and personal lives—it's the bond that ties people together.

The Key to the Knight's Success: Loyalty

Loyalty isn't grey. It's black and white.
You're either loyal completely, or not loyal at
all. And people have to understand this. You
can't be loyal only when it serves you.

—Sharnay

Knights are protectors, champions, defenders of and believers in their missions and the organizations they work for, the people they work with—and even in their customers. Our knights are loyal.

As a leader, when you have the persona of a knight, your employees feel safe when you protect and serve them. And when they feel safe, they can make bold moves as individuals— moves that can lead your business to new opportunities and successes. Loyalty is about bonding and protecting; it is about acting as a unit—a partnership—providing security for one another, giving emotional support when necessary, and protecting those who work for us, as well as the people for whom we work.

But loyalty is more than just working together and being bonded to one another. It's about pooling the talents and strengths of others in ways that make people feel stronger. People who work in organizations are human beings who want to contribute and belong—they want to know they are defending something meaningful. Most people who take the time to go to work each day don't do it just for a paycheck—they go to work each day because they want to devote their minds to something meaningful, and they want their hearts to resonate with something purposeful.

The knight knows how to release the spark within his people and earn their loyalty.

According to loyalty expert James Kane, "Loyalty is all in your head"—no different from the other emotions we experience as human beings, including happiness, sadness, love, and hate.

Kane says, "And just like any emotion, it is a result of our brain's response to certain stimuli. Our mind sees, hears, feels, or senses all sorts of things that trigger very specific emotional reactions in us, typically followed by some correlated behavior."[9]

According to Kane, three specific things determine whether or not we feel a sense of loyalty to another person, product, brand, or organization. These three things are:

A sense of trust. Trust is the foundation on which we build loyalty. If we don't trust that someone will be consistent in his or her behavior and actions, then the loyalty we feel may be fleeting.

A sense of belonging. When we feel a sense of belonging, we feel a personal connection to another person, product, brand, or organization. We identify with someone or something, and we solidify the bonds between us through our loyalty.

A sense of purpose. When CEOs paint an inspiring vision of the future, they create a sense of purpose that draws people to them, and to their product, brand, and organization—and it earns their loyalty.

As Kane puts it, "We want our leaders to be like us, to think like us, and to act the way we would."[10] We all aspire to be knights, and we give our loyalty to the knights among us.

How can you spot a knight in your organization?

The knight as a leader is always in service to others. Knights serve with the twin ideals of loyalty and devotion. They view things in terms of, "How can I help you get this job done?"—knowing that if they pull their weight, others will pull theirs just as fiercely, and with just as much devotion.

The knight knows that loyalty is about reliability. When reliability is present, people feel empowered. Yes, people are stronger when they are together. But if you knew that you had someone who is looking out for you—watching your back—you just might feel *invincible*.

The knight has a fierce determination to be committed to his people. When leaders are fully committed to their people, the determination employees feel within is fierce. When a leader takes the stand, "I will do *anything* for my people," employees feel empowered to take chances.

The knight demonstrates competencies. Leaders must be competent in their skills—they must master the knowledge required in their positions, have good judgment, and demonstrate significant abilities. Leaders must also have strong character and be decisive. Their courage and confidence must be unquestioned, and they must set an exemplary example for others to follow.

For the knight, loyalty is defined as a commitment or an allegiance to a person, a group, or a cause. A knight is capable, charismatic, charming, daring, dignified, and dutiful. He has strong opinions, and an even stronger mind, and yet he leads with a tender heart.

The Knight's Leadership Gap: Self-Serving

Of course the self-serving bias is something you want to get out of yourself. Thinking that what's good for you is good for the wider civilization and rationalizing all these ridiculous conclusions based on this subconscious tendency to serve one's self is a terribly inaccurate way to think.

—Charlie Munger

I was summoned to assist an industrial conglomerate located in a large Asian capital. The company was experiencing a surge in growth at a time when many similar companies were shrinking. The business's leadership accomplished this growth through very smart strategies, including expanding the company's portfolio through lightning-fast acquisitions of its competitors.

My job was to ensure a smooth transition for one of the new acquisitions by coaching that company's CEO, Francesca, on how to integrate well with the new parent company.

The transition would take up to two years, and Francesca would need the help and support of many people—in particular, the former CEO of the newly acquired company, Lin. The parent company had made a sweet deal—giving Lin a handsome payout, but also asked him to stay on for up to two years as a paid consultant to help the new CEO with the transition.

When the acquisition team conducted due diligence, everyone at the company seemed friendly, eager, and excited about the change. But as soon as the sale was finalized, the story became entirely different.

Lin began to shut his door whenever Francesca was around, and was always busy when the new CEO wanted to talk to him. Not only that, but in meetings, he openly criticized Francesca, making fun of the way she spoke. He mimicked her thick French accent, saying, "I don't understand you—can you please speak in English?" He couldn't let any opportunity to belittle Francesca pass by.

At first, Francesca—my client—did not know how to react to his slights. She felt betrayed, and she was extremely concerned. During our coaching call, she said, "I need Lin's support to be successful. Without him, I cannot do this. I moved my entire family here, and frankly, I am not about to fail."

I reassured her, saying, "We just have to work with the situation we have, and we will do everything possible to make it work. The first thing you must do is find out what is going on. Call a meeting for the two of you to get to the bottom of this."

When the meeting was finally scheduled, after many back-and-forth calls, Francesca breathed a sigh of relief. But shortly before the meeting, Lin canceled. He sent a note saying that he was too busy and that they should reschedule as soon as possible. Days turned into weeks, and still the meeting was not rescheduled. Each time Francesca walked into Lin's office, he waved her away—promising he would catch her later.

We finally came up with an idea. Francesca invited Lin and his wife to dinner at her new home with her husband. Lin accepted. The dinner turned out to be cordial and gracious, convincing Francesca that she had finally earned the loyalty and support she sought.

But it did not last. Within a few days, Francesca noticed that Lin was back to his old ways—serving himself and not the company. He was calling in his top people and having meetings with them at all hours of the day. At first, Francesca tried to give him the benefit of the doubt—hoping he was just reining in the old troops. But when trips to visit new clients were being scheduled without her involvement, she knew this had to stop.

"This isn't working," she told me during our next coaching session. "I don't understand—I am willing to work with him, but he isn't willing to work with me. He is sabotaging the entire acquisition and the opportunity to grow—I have too much riding on this."

"Why don't you talk to Lin's top people," I suggested, "and find out what their gripes are? They need to understand that Lin will be leaving eventually, and in order to be successful, they will have to be loyal and not self-serving. You have to make them part of the change initiative and the redesign of the organization. Give them prominent positions and let their voices be heard. The only way for you to succeed is to have them on board, and you must earn their loyalty."

And so Francesca called a meeting with Lin's top people. It didn't go well. Their loyalty was with their old boss, and they were not motivated to change. It was apparent that those who could help with the transition—those who could make the two companies successful as one—were not going to help.

My client was extremely frustrated. "How can I make it work," she asked, "when those men and women are so loyal to their old boss?"

Clearly there was only one solution.

"Lin has to leave," I coached her, "and he has to leave *now*. Not in the next few weeks, months, or years—in the next few days. He cannot participate in the transition—period."

Francesca appealed to the board of directors. Eventually they agreed to the termination of the former CEO, effective immediately.

True to form, some members of Lin's loyal team followed him out of the company, while others stayed. Francesca told those who stayed that self-serving attitudes would not be tolerated. With Lin out of the picture, she quickly earned the respect and loyalty of the company's executives and employees, and the transition proceeded smoothly.

I have seen a distinct pattern in organizations of all sizes and in every industry: The companies that lack loyal leaders have the most difficult time hiring and retaining talented people. A recent survey of human resources professionals and hiring managers conducted by CareerBuilder revealed that approximately one in five employees (22 percent) do not feel loyal to their current employer and are planning to leave their current position and change jobs within a year.[11]

According to a previous CareerBuilder survey,[12] some of the reasons given for this disloyalty include:

"Don't feel my employer values me."

"Employer does not pay enough."

"My efforts are not recognized or appreciated."

"Not enough career advancement opportunities."

Loyal employees become disloyal one infraction at a time. Many leaders do not even notice when disloyalty or self-serving attitudes develop in their colleagues, associates, or peers, because it is a slow, subtle unraveling. Only after unfaithfulness shapes itself does the self-serving attitude emerge in a way it can be detected and deciphered.

Embracing a self-serving attitude as a virtue means trashing any hope of love, friendship, and community—the things that bring the most fundamental joy and satisfaction to our lives.

The Knight's Leadership Gap Archetype: The Mercenary

> Smart people instinctively understand the dangers of entrusting our future to self-serving leaders who use our institutions— whether in the corporate or social sectors—to advance their own interests.
>
> —James C. Collins

The leadership gap of the knight is a mercenary leader who cares not about serving others but only about serving himself. When the knight asks, "Who can I serve?" the mercenary leader asks, **"How can I serve myself?"**

Mercenary leaders are always all about *them*. If a leader doesn't understand that leadership is about serving others, then they will not engender loyalty from those they lead. Anyone who leads by self-absorption or self-obsession is a leader who will not succeed.

Mercenary leaders have the following qualities:

Lack of dedication. When you have leaders who are not invested in those they lead—when they don't support or coach their colleagues, or guide and mentor their team—this shows disinterest. A leader who is not committed to the growth and development of others is not fully invested in his people's success. A loyal leader knows the importance of investing in the development of his people, because leadership is all about being committed to your people. The way we treat others will determine our own success or failure.

Inadequate loyalty. When leaders don't protect, safeguard, or defend their people, the people do not feel secure. Security is important—if there is no safety there is no loyalty. Just saying to someone, "You should feel secure," "Your job is safe," or "You can rely on me" doesn't make someone dedicated and loyal to you or your organization. The best leaders demonstrate loyalty first by letting employees know they have their back and will protect them. That is what loyal leaders do.

Absence of accountability. When leaders are not accountable for their mistakes and failures, they tend to blame others—including those who work for them. This breeds disloyalty among employees. The best leaders know that loyalty is earned through everyday actions and everyday decisions because everything a leader says and does has consequences.

Shortage of competence. When leaders lack focus and have a hard time paying attention to details, they come across as leaders who are not competent. Leaders who cannot deliver on their obligations will not only be unsuccessful, but they will lose the faithfulness of their followers. Leadership is about performance—it is about starting something and getting the job done.

Loyalty isn't gray; it's black or white. Either you are completely loyal or you are not loyal at all.

Leveraging the Mercenary Within

> A true warrior can only serve others, not
> himself. . . . When you become a
> mercenary, you're just a bully with a gun.
> —Evan Wright

Bridging the gap between being a knight who is loyal and the mercenary who is self-serving requires an understanding that leaders come from a place of dedication, devotion, and duty. Great leaders do not boast, do not seek titles, and do not need to keep a personal ledger of who has done right and who has done wrong.

The knight leader honors and protects people and champions for them, while doing battle for honorable causes. Knights serve with loyalty, and they get loyalty in return. The knight knows that loyalty isn't just the idea that someone has your back; it's the idea that people can trust him—on bad days and good. Why? Because they know his record and they have seen his dedication. To protect and preserve is the best guarantee of a knight because the love he has for his people and the honorable cause is what drives him. The knight does not want to do what is easy; he wants to do what is right. When things are going well for a business, it's easy to be loyal. But when things become challenging, loyalty gets tested, and that is when true loyalty prevails.

Being a mercenary might feel like an easier path to

leadership, but at their core, great leaders know that the key to their success is serving others first—not themselves. A leadership gap is created when someone thinks that he should serve himself first and everyone else after. For leaders who have this bias, making the change isn't easy—it requires first rethinking what is truly best for the organization, and ultimately for themselves. Understand that leading requires others to follow—we don't lead in a vacuum. To succeed, we must become the kind of leader who serves others first and not ourselves.

Pay attention to how people respond to you. If you take a second to stop focusing exclusively on *you,* you will be able to tell if someone is feeling upset, annoyed, or just plain frustrated. Pay attention to their tone of voice and whether their answers are curt or short. These are telltale indications that they are not responding to you or how you are behaving. Listen to what other people say, and put the focus more on them in your conversations.

Put yourself in the other person's shoes. Not everything is about you—many things are about others. A mercenary is self-serving, so it's important to really listen to what others are saying and try to absorb anything they tell you. This may seem like common sense, but when some of us are in a conversation, we are just hearing the words people are saying and not really understanding or listening. Try putting yourself in someone else's shoes. Be empathetic, compassionate, and understanding. This will keep you from coming across as self-serving.

Get to know the people around you. Do what you can to

connect deeply with people, get to know them, and be sincerely interested in them. When people show an interest in you, show an interest back. When you connect with others, others will connect with you. Not everything in the world revolves around you.

Whatever actions you take, think of others and not just yourself. Whatever it is that you do and whatever actions you take, don't do it just to accomplish a self-serving goal—think of how it could benefit others. By having this mentality, you are bound to find others who are willing to help you and aid you in your cause. Not only that, the actions you take will be done for the greater good of many and will be much more rewarding once your goals are accomplished.

When you stop serving yourself and you start serving others, you will experience what it means to finally find purpose for your greatness.

Becoming a Knight Leader

Knighthood lies above eternity; it doesn't
live off fame, but rather deeds.

—Dejan Stojanović

Becoming a great leader is much more than just being capable in your job. While competence is an important part of the leadership equation, interpersonal skills are just as important.

You must connect with your people on a personal level and exhibit authentic care for others. Moreover, knight leaders allow their people to reciprocate this care. The best leaders know they cannot ignore the needs and aspirations of their team. There has to be a bond and an understanding between the two, and leaders who invest time in creating this bond are rewarded with the loyalty of their people in return.

The path to greatness for the knight is direct:

Articulate an authentic vision. When a leader creates and communicates a compelling vision—grounded in a worthy cause that speaks to the heart of his people—employees will always be energized by and loyal to that vision.

Walk your talk. Great leaders believe actions speak louder than words. They understand that the power lies within those who can walk their talk, and lead by example, because within their example, the importance of loyalty is clear, precise, powerful, and authentic.

Listen intently. Truly great leaders understand that listening to their people, knowing what they want from their lives—at work and at home—and knowing what drives them and sparks their passion and engagement is one of the best ways to get their loyalty.

Be honest with yourself. You can't expect your employees to be loyal to you if you aren't being honest with yourself and acting with integrity. Loyalty breeds loyalty, just as dishonesty breeds dishonesty. Be truthful with your employees, even if it hurts. Respect comes when your employees know that it costs you something to be honest with them.

Care for your employees. Get to know your employees as

people first, and then as workers. Seek opportunities to connect with them on a personal level. Get to know their interests, hobbies, aspirations, and goals. Your company's most valuable asset is not the services it provides or the products it makes—it's the people it employs.

Respect others. As a knight, you must show others respect by offering the best of who you are. Give your people your respect by not withholding crucial information or responsibilities from them. To earn respect and loyalty from your people, you must first give it to them. Empower them to make decisions and encourage their growth and opportunities.

Lead only with the best. Loyalty is not leading with everyone; loyalty is leading with the *best*. The selection of employees is just as important as the selection of customers. It's easier to get into Harvard or Princeton than it is to be hired by Southwest Airlines, which hired only 2 percent of the 371,202 people who applied for jobs last year.[13] Where you choose to work is just as important as whom you serve.

GREAT KNIGHT LEADERS

Mother Teresa, whose loyalty to the Catholic Church and the impoverished people she served was unwavering, even as she questioned her faith in God.

Herb Kelleher, who founded Southwest Airlines and created a unique company culture that was both low-cost and fun for employees—and for the intensely loyal customers who fly the airline in droves.

Jill Abramson, who spent her career working her way up from Washington Bureau Chief to the executive editor of the *New York Times*. The company fired her with much fanfare, and she has yet to say a bad word about them.

The knight serves in many ways. When you offer your people opportunity, title, and position, you expect them to honor those roles. And loyalty is earned.

When you bring all of who you are—with the best of your skills and abilities—then loyalty is earned.

When you create a team that is bonded, and whose members affirm their commitments to one another for the good of themselves—and for the good of the organization—then loyalty is earned.

Lead with reciprocal loyalty and service. And be mindful should your service ever become self-serving. When you lead as a knight, your greatness has profound meaning.

Recognizing Yourself in the Knight Archetype

The knight lives by loyalty and the pride of protecting people and preserving admirable goals.

Are you a knight? Ask yourself these questions:

- Why is being of service to others important to you?

- Why do you feel that protecting others is a big part of who you are?

- What is your personal code of honor?

- Do others consider you to be arrogant or self-serving? Why?

- How do you react to selfishness and self-serving people?

CHAPTER NINE

WHERE THERE IS LIGHT THERE IS ALWAYS HOPE FOR GREATNESS

Hope is being able to see that there is light despite all of the darkness.

—Desmond Tutu

Most of us believe that a leader who exhibits confidence, who has faith in his intuition, who speaks with candor, who leads with courage and integrity, and who cultivates trust and loyalty is a rare find.

But I hope I have convinced you that there are many great leaders among us, and recognizing them is a bit easier now. You are surrounded by rebels, explorers, truth tellers, heroes, inventors, navigators, and knights. Do you see them now?

Working with hundreds of organizations—big and small, in every industry, and all around the world—I have trained thousands of leaders in how to overcome their leadership gaps and achieve greatness. Most come to understand that mission is more important than profit, that people are more important than process, that money can be made in ways that don't exploit others, and that making a positive influence on society—and the world—is not only feasible but rewarding.

Sometimes we have to see it to believe it; sometimes we have to understand it to comprehend it; and sometimes we just have to experience it to see the wisdom in it.

City of Hope is a private, not-for-profit hospital, clinical research center, and graduate medical school primarily located on a 110-acre campus just outside Los Angeles in Duarte, California. The organization was founded by a group of volunteers who chartered the Jewish Consumptive Relief Association in 1913 to fight the spread of tuberculosis by establishing a free nonsectarian sanatorium. The sanatorium was originally just two canvas cottages on ten acres of land purchased by the group.

As the sanatorium grew, it gained the nickname "the city of hope"—and its mission expanded beyond tuberculosis to other diseases. Today City of Hope is one of the world's preeminent cancer centers, and the organization has been on the front lines of the fights against diabetes and HIV/AIDS. Throughout it all, City of Hope has held true to its humanitarian vision that "health is a human right." In the spirit of that vision, Samuel H. Golter—one of City of Hope's early leaders—coined the phrase "There is no profit in curing the body if, in the process, we destroy the soul."

And these words became City of Hope's credo and weighed heavily on Robert W. Stone's heart when he came to the campus one afternoon. He didn't know it right then, but one day he would become City of Hope's CEO.

Robert W. Stone is a native of Southern California, raised

in Whittier. He attended the University of Redlands and played basketball there for four seasons, earning a bachelor's degree in political science. He was named to the Academic All-America team by the College Sports Information Directors of America and ranks fifteenth at Redlands in career points scored, with 1,077. "I never envisioned being a CEO," he said. "I went to Redlands to play basketball."[1]

Robert went on to earn a law degree at the University of Chicago and returned to California after he graduated to practice business law. "Chicago was so cold. I froze and came back here," he said. "There's no way to prepare for 40 below."[2] Early in his career, Robert decided to join a small firm in Southern California near where he had grown up. Two years later, he received a call from someone who worked in the general counsel's office at City of Hope. "We need help," said the caller. "I need you to come." Robert had heard of City of Hope, but he didn't know anyone who was affiliated with the organization. Robert told the caller no, not once but twice. But the person from the general counsel's office was persistent, and he tried one more time.

"If I buy you lunch in the cafeteria," he asked Robert, "would you just come in for an interview?"

Robert was planning to decline once more, but after their meal they walked the grounds of City of Hope and two things struck Robert:

We came around a corner by the rose garden, and on the gate there is penned a motto by one of my predecessors: "There is no profit in curing the body if, in the process, we destroy the soul." That really caught my attention, but right after that I went around the corner and there was a nurse pulling a red wagon with a bald-headed, three-year-old child in it. The child was smiling and feeling good, and the kid's mother was following behind—pushing an IV pump for her child. She was crying profusely. To this day I don't know if she was crying because she was sad, or because she was so happy. Maybe it was the first time in a long time that her child felt good enough to be out in the sunlight. Either way, this caught my attention, and it became an aha moment for me. I realized that this is a place where I can make a difference.[3]

And Robert said yes.

Robert was hired as City of Hope's associate general counsel, and in the twenty years he's been with the organization, he has held eleven different positions—culminating in his current job as CEO. While he is now fully in charge of the operation, Robert's main focus is on the patients and their care. Robert says, "I can say we are going to get market share or we are going to have better access for our patients—one of these messages inspires and one does not. At City of Hope, everyone is part of the mission, purpose, and vision. Everyone feels they are playing a part."

For Robert, what City of Hope does is stay true to the credo he read the first day he walked onto its campus.

For City of Hope, what is most important are the people—the researchers, the doctors, the nurses, the patients, the caretakers, and the community. City of Hope is all about service and serving with heart.

When you listen to Robert W. Stone talk about City of Hope today, you cannot help but be moved by the organization's mission, its purpose, and the acts of not-so-small kindness they do every day:

> There are many different parts of the City of Hope, but the overriding umbrella is the unwavering dedication to serving humanity. At City of Hope, whether you are in patient services, a nurse, a valet, a doctor, a leader, a researcher—it doesn't matter. You have to be willing to make yourself smaller than the greater good. And the people who do well here, in this community are not here for themselves, people are here because they want to give back to their fellow man.[4]

By staying true to that mission over the years, City of Hope has moved to the front line in the global battle against cancer and other life-threatening diseases. They're proud to say that they are able to do something very special for the patients who are their customers: to combine science with soul to create miracles that make lives whole again. And for Robert, this is the ultimate reward. "I am a lucky man," he says. "City of Hope has taught me what it truly means to give back."

As an organization, City of Hope is empirical proof that it is possible to run a business that is successful while it serves.

Moreover, Robert W. Stone demonstrates that to be a

highly effective leader, you don't have to be outspoken, filled with power, ego-driven, self-centered, or a bully. Robert W. Stone leads as a gentle warrior. He understands that the mission and vision of his organizations are the driver. He acknowledges that *people* are what matter most, and he does it all with a humble heart.

In a world where everything always has to be faster, better, brighter, Robert exemplifies why the gentle warrior, the quiet soul, is the right kind of leaders. If you speak with Robert, you'll quickly realize that he is no pushover—he is smart in his strategy, he is a visionary in his thinking, and he encompasses and epitomizes all of the archetypes presented in this book.

Robert embodies the best of every archetype: he's a rebel with confidence; an explorer who is intuitive; a truth teller who speaks with candor; a hero who has courage; an inventor who works with integrity; a navigator who guides his organization ever forward; and a knight who is loyal to his people. Robert's mission, his purpose, and his vision are not focused only on his business today, but on the quality of health care that will be delivered long into the future.

As a leader, even each small choice you make has great impact, and determines outcomes for you, your people, your organization, your community, and for the world as a whole. Robert W. Stone appreciates the gravity of that fact.

You might not see him or read about him, or catch him on your nightly news, but for those in need, he delivers; for those who call for him, he shows up; for those who count on him, he is trusted. He demonstrates confidence, loyalty, and integrity every day. For those who look to Robert W. Stone as their leader, this makes a world of difference.

His success goes way beyond profits and metrics of returns. Robert W. Stone's leadership is memorable and admirable—something that most leaders strive to achieve but don't know how.

His presence is felt, his wisdom is acknowledged, and his heart is there for all to see.

The quiet ones, the humble ones, the gentle warriors—those are the leaders we have to learn from; they are the ones who give us hope.

Being a leader isn't easy—it's filled with challenges, complications, and consequences, and it has a way of testing us each and every day. And with each challenge, we have to do what we can to succeed—to not engage is to fail.

Everything we do and say ends up being our message to the world. We have to be vigilant with the words we speak and the example we set. Do we lead with light, or are we leading with shadows? What messages are we sending?

If we lead with positivity, we will get an organization that is heartfelt and positive.

If we lead with negativity, we will have an organization that also reflects that negativity.

If you think your behaviors and your actions don't matter, then think again. If you think you can deny or dismiss the shadows within you, then take a moment to rethink what you believe. Who we are always stays with us: the good and the bad, the light and the dark, the weak and the strong.

If you think you can fake it till you make it, then think again.

If you think no one is watching you as you lead, then think again.

If you think you can compress it or constrict it, then think again.

We have to be cognizant and vigilant of who we are at all times. You cannot, and should not, try to segregate the parts within—the good and the bad—that make us a complete leader. Your weaknesses create the leadership gap within you, but you cannot be a complete leader without acknowledging and working with the polarities within your leadership. Your entire life—your meaning and your purpose—is about unifying who you are in the process of becoming the best leader possible.

If you want to get your leadership right, you have to get *yourself* right. But first you must take this message of rethinking everything you think you know to heart—no matter how frightening or frustrating it might be to you. Decades ago, Erich Fromm warned us that nothing radical, scary, or frightening would be able to survive unless we embodied it, unless we made it our message, unless we lived it.

How will you live your leadership archetypes? How will you embody them, engage them, and embrace them? How will you make this message a part of your leadership, and a part of who you are? When you put the knowledge I have imparted in this book to work, it will not only give you hope—it will give you the tools and the sensibilities to understand that you have within you the fundamental principles that can make you great.

Your greatness is not a function of circumstances. Greatness, as it turns out, lies within your leadership gaps and knowing how to leverage them. You have the power within you not to be imprisoned by your circumstances, or jailed by your setbacks, or shackled by your mistakes, or beaten by your defeats. Every single one of us has the chance and the choice to choose to stand in our greatness or not.

What will you do?

EPILOGUE:
STAND IN YOUR GREATNESS

True greatness consists in being great in little
things.

—Charles Simmons

Understanding your leadership archetype is just the beginning of rethinking who you are and who you are being when you are leading. Each of us was put on this earth to achieve our greatest self, and by working through this process it will not only help you discover your leadership gaps, but it will help you identify what is keeping you from your greatness.

If greatness is what you want, then you must *choose* greatness, because it will allow you to reap the reward of having more meaning in your life, deeper purpose in your work, and the self-permission to be the person you are meant to be. Greatness is a lot of small things done very well every day. Here are some proven approaches to take your leadership and life past your leadership gaps and onto the next level:

For Yourself

1. Be transparent and open. Discovering and leveraging your leadership archetype will be easier and more accurate when you are willing to open yourself up to an honest self-examination of your true personality and motivations.

2. Build bridges of trust. You need the trust and support of your people to succeed as a leader. Instead of tearing down bridges of trust, build them up.

3. Be willing to take risks. Great leadership takes bravery and a willingness to take risks—and encouraging your people to take risks, too. When lessons are learned from failure, they can be our best teachers. You don't have to be great to take risks; you just have to risk to be great.

4. Celebrate your victories. In a business world that is busier and more complex than ever, it's important to step back for a moment to celebrate your victories. This will give you the time you need to recharge your batteries to take on the next challenge . . . and the next, and the next.

5. Don't try to do it all yourself. Delegation is the number one tool of every great leader. Hire the right people, train them well, then delegate your organization's work to them. Save the things that only you can do for yourself—otherwise, let it go. If you want to achieve greatness, stop doing everything alone.

6. Make it a habit to respect everyone. Be the kind of leader people admire. Respect people, trust people, and have the confidence in yourself to lead with heart.

7. Take responsibility for your problems; don't blame others. All of us have experiences that have caused us problems. But to truly make a positive impact, we have to take responsibility for what we went through in the past, while being accountable for the future. When you blame others you give up your power to make a positive impact.

8. Spend time with people who are important to you. Make the important relationships in your life a priority. Good relationships don't just happen—they take time and patience. Make a positive impact on a life by making it a priority.

9. Praise someone at work for a job well done. When the occasion arises, praise people. Praise means you are acknowledging and appreciating. What you praise you increase; that is, you get more of the behavior that sparked your praise in the first place. Your work, fame, and position cannot reveal the greatness of your soul. Only your kindness can do that.

10. Listen to people with interest, concern, and compassion. The leaders who have the greatest impact give people their full attention. All people want is someone who will listen— someone who pays attention and someone who shows concern and compassion. The leaders who make a difference are not the ones with the best credentials, but the ones with the most concern.

11. Develop your character. Your character will be defined by what you do when you think no one is looking. Good character is to be admired more than outstanding talent. Your talents are a gift, but your character by contrast is about your choice and determination. Never settle for being an average person—you were made for greatness.

12. Pay it forward. Take time out of your busy day to stop for a moment and think how you can pay it forward. No one can help everyone, but everyone can help someone. Your greatness is not what you have; it's what you give.

For Your People

1. Share your leadership. Give your people opportunities to grow in their careers while gaining self-confidence and experience, by sharing your leadership duties with them.

2. Recognize and reward your people. When your people do great work, be sure to recognize and reward the effort. Remember: you get what you reward.

3. Set the bar high. Encourage and expect excellence from your people, and create high standards that require them to stretch to meet those goals. Not only will your organization benefit as a result, but so will your people.

4. Pay them well. If you want to attract and retain the very best people, you've got to pay them a higher wage than your competitors do. Keep a close eye on what your competition is paying their people, and stay a step ahead.

5. Insist on accountability. When your employees agree to take on a task or achieve a goal, hold them to their commitment. If you don't hold your people accountable for their promises, then some won't bother fulfilling them.

6. A point of view isn't enough—make what you know teachable. The difference between a good leader and a great leader is the ability to teach and coach people. If you seek greatness, be the kind of leader who provides a baseline for your coaching and teachable points of view.

7. Encourage someone to believe in himself. We all know those times when we lose our confidence. Be the person who can empower someone.

8. Don't judge others. Before you assume, learn the facts. Before you judge, understand. Before you speak, think.

9. Leverage your past experiences. The best leaders consciously think about their experiences and rethink what they know and what they need to learn. The greatest leaders teach from their experiences while telling compelling stories that help people make the right decisions and take the right actions.

10. Write a thank-you note when someone does something nice for you. Letting your people know how much you appreciate their generosity will go miles. This extra effort leaves lasting goodwill in its wake.

11. Give credit where credit is due. Whether you are a supervisor or a subordinate, it's essential for workplace morale that you acknowledge and commend efficiency, hard work, and initiative. Thanking employees privately isn't always enough. Praising them in front of others, writing a letter for their personnel file, or presenting them with an award are ways to show that their efforts have not gone unnoticed.

12. Help make dreams come true. The next time someone shares a goal or a dream they have, really encourage them to pursue it—requesting that they take some kind of action within a certain time frame. Then, if they agree to a date to fulfill their goal, make sure to follow up with them when that date arrives.

For Your Community

1. Provide opportunities for volunteerism. Give your employees opportunities to volunteer in the communities in which you do business, by connecting them with local nonprofits and providing paid time off to serve.

2. Be a good citizen. Give back to your community in every way you can, whenever you can.

3. Hire locally. Whenever possible, focus your hiring efforts in your community. Provide ample training opportunities so that your employees can advance in the organization.

4. Feed the homeless. See something, do something. Don't walk past the homeless. Buy a homeless person a real meal—don't give them your leftovers.

5. Share your expertise. Contribute your talents and lend your specialty to your community.

6. Rescue an animal. Find a pet at the Humane Society. You can even search for a place to rescue animals in your local community.

7. Attend a city council meeting. Let your voice be heard. Speak up honestly and bravely. Stand for a cause. Have a purpose. Make it meaningful.

8. Mentor a child. Educate and encourage children to become leaders. It will teach them to care for others.

9. Build a home for Habitat for Humanity. Help build a home for those in need. The best kind of charity starts in your own backyard.

10. Lead a project for a nonprofit. Perhaps you can collect needed items, make crafts to donate, organize an outing for people in need, or sponsor a celebration of some sort with the organization.

11. Take care of the planet. Plant a tree or flowers in your community; recycle paper, plastics, and cans. Educate people on how to care for the planet.

12. Be the solution. Observe your environment, find a problem, and come up with the solution.

Start today. Look for your gaps. Leverage your gaps. And stand in your greatness.

Assessment

If you want to learn about what gets between you and your greatness, take your assessment today:

www.lollydaskal/assessment

KNOW YOUR GAPS AND UNLEASH YOUR
GREATNESS

LEADERSHIP ARCHETYPE	LEADERSHIP STYLE	LEADERSHIP GAP	UNLEASH YOUR GREATNESS
REBEL	Leads with confidence and self-assurance.	Impostors are fueled by their self-doubt.	Leverage your competencies and capabilities to boost your confidence.
EXPLORER	Seeks to discover new opportunities and experiences. Uses intuition to move forward.	Exploiters manipulate people to exert control.	Leverage your instincts to take back control.
TRUTH TELLER	Speaks with candor, willing to pay a big price for telling the truth.	Deceivers create suspicion by withholding information.	Leverage candor. Lead with veracity. Speak your truth.
HERO	Demonstrates courage in spite of fears and apprehension.	Bystanders see things and do nothing, hear things and say nothing.	Leverage courage by resisting your fears.
INVENTOR	Performs with integrity and high standards to produce excellence.	Destroyers are corrupt by cutting corners and looking for fast, cheap ways of getting things done.	Leverage your integrity and standards to lead with excellence.
NAVIGATOR	Steers people to find practical and pragmatic solutions for challenging and complex problems.	Fixers who want to help situations and people often come across as arrogant.	Leverage your problem-solving skills without imposing yourself on others.
KNIGHT	Strong sense of duty to be loyal and protective of others.	Mercenaries always serve themselves first.	Leverage your sense of duty in the service of others and make everything larger and more pronounced.

ACKNOWLEDGMENTS

Nothing great has ever been achieved without great people.

To my three children, Michaela, Ariel, and Zoe, who taught me that you don't have to be great to start, but you have to start to be great.

To Peter Economy, who believed in me enough to say let's make this happen. And stayed with me every step of the way to make sure it happened. Your craft, guidance, and brilliance not only made this book possible but helped me accomplish the impossible.

To Kristi Faulkner, who took my complicated thoughts and knew exactly how to simplify them, because everything meaningful should be made as simple as possible, but not simpler.

To Frank Sonnenberg, who taught me that true friendship means to stand by when everything seems like it's falling into the gaps.

To Michael Wade, who generously added his two cents, which were priceless.

ACKNOWLEDGMENTS

To Giles Anderson, who knows that a great book isn't born until a great agent gives birth to it.

To Jesse Maeshiro, whose dedication, feedback, and time will always be greatly appreciated.

To Eric Nelson, who believed greatness was to be found and helped me to find it.

To John Anderson, whose dedication taught me that to be a great leader, you must first become a great person.

To Frances Hesselbein, who proved that really great people make you feel that you, too, can become great.

To Ester Fuchs, who saw how every great solution needs a great problem.

To Daniel Lubetzky, who demonstrates that kindness will always advance greatness.

To Viktor Frankl, Carl Jung, and Joseph Campbell, who teach that great men and women are not born great, they develop greatness.

To my clients, who show me that greatness lies within everyone.

To all my gaps: I thank you, because without you, I would never be the person I am today.

NOTES

INTRODUCTION
1. Joseph Campbell, *Reflections on the Art of Living* (Harper Perennial, 1995).
2. Interview with Joseph Campbell, cited in https://mappalicious .com/2014/04/02/bibliophilia-how-reading-and-writing-can -save-our-soul/

CHAPTER ONE: THE SURPRISING GAP IN OUR LEADERSHIP
1. Vickor Frankl, *Man's Search for Meaning* (Pocket Books, 1997), p. 86.
2. Alex Pattakos, *Prisoners of Our Thoughts: Viktor Frankl's Principles for Discovering Meaning in Life and Work, 2nd Ed.* (Berrett-Koehler, 2010).

CHAPTER TWO: THE REBEL
1. Barbara Arneil, "Gender, Diversity, and Organizational Change: The Boy Scouts vs. Girl Scouts of America," *Perspectives on Politics*, March 2010, pp. 53–68.
2. Sally Helgesen, "Frances Hesselbein's Merit Badge in Leadership," *strategy+business*, May 11, 2015.

3. Jim Collins, foreword for *Hesselbein on Leadership* (Jossey-Bass, 2002).

4. Personal interview with Peter Economy, May 2005.

5. Collins, foreword for *Hesselbein on Leadership*.

6. Sally Helgesen, "Frances Hesselbein's Merit Badge in Leadership."

7. Arneil, "Gender, Diversity, and Organizational Change."

8. Tomas Chamorro-Premuzic, PhD, *Confidence: How Much You Really Need and How to Get It* (Hudson Street Press, 2013), p. 1.

CHAPTER THREE: THE EXPLORER

1. www.cleanclothes.org/ranaplaza/who-needs-to-pay-up

2. www.globallabourrights.org/alerts/rana-plaza-bangladesh
-anniversary-a-look-back-and-forward

3. www.theguardian.com/world/2013/apr/26/bangladesh-building
-official-response-fury

4. www.huffingtonpost.com/shannon-whitehead/5-truths-the-fast
-fashion_b_5690575.html

5. www.dailymail.co.uk/home/you/article-2585166/Safia-Minney
-founder-fair-trade-label-People-Tree-shares-treasures.html

6. www.theguardian.com/lifeandstyle/2010/jun/13/shahesta
-shaitly-five-things-know-about-style-safia-minney-people-tree

7. http://www.peopletree.co.uk/about-us

8. Mary Goulet, *Go with Your Gut: How to Make Decisions You Can Trust* (Mary Goulet Media, 2011).

9. Granville Toogood, *The Creative Executive: How Business Leaders Innovate by Stimulating Passion, Intuition, and Creativity to Develop Fresh Ideas* (Adams Media Corporation, 2000), p. 57.

10. Gary Klein, *Sources of Power: How People Make Decisions* (The MIT Press, 1999), p. 34.

11. Ron Nelson, "How to Be a Manager," *Success*, July–August 1985, p. 69.

12. Stephen Harper, "Intuition: What Separates Executives from Managers," *Business Horizons* 31, no. 5, p. 15.

CHAPTER FOUR: THE TRUTH TELLER

1. www.azcentral.com/story/money/business/super-bowl/2015/01
   /30/nfls-financial-success-draws-scrutiny-controversy
   /22585761/
2. www.azcentral.com/story/money/business/super-bowl/2015/01
   /30/nfls-financial-success-draws-scrutiny-controversy
   /22585761/
3. www.slate.com/articles/sports/sports_nut/2015/12/the_truth
   _about_will_smith_s_concussion_and_bennet_omalu.html
4. Jeanne Marie Laskas, "Game Brain," *GQ*, September 14, 2009.
5. Les Carpenter, "'Brain Chaser' Tackles Effects of NFL Hits,"
   The Washington Post, April 25, 2007.
6. http://www.pbs.org/wgbh/frontline/article/the-autopsy-that
   -changed-football/
7. http://www.pbs.org/wgbh/frontline/film/league-of-denial
   /transcript/
8. Laskas, "Game Brain."
9. Ibid.
10. http://onlyagame.wbur.org/2015/12/19/concussion-football-omalu
    -movie
11. Laskas, "Game Brain."
12. www.nfl.com/news/story/0ap1000000235501/article/nfl-retired
    -players-agree-to-concussion-lawsuit-settlement
13. www.cbsnews.com/news/concussion-movie-doctors-speak-out
    -nfl-cte/
14. http://mentalfloss.com/article/30609/60-people-cant-go-10
    -minutes-without-lying
15. http://usatoday30.usatoday.com/news/health/story/2012-08-04
    /honesty-beneficial-to-health/56782648/1

CHAPTER FIVE: THE HERO

1. http://www.pbs.org/wgbh/americanexperience/features
   /transcript/henryford-transcript/

2. Ibid.

3. Ibid.

4. www.telegraph.co.uk/news/science/science-news/7850263/Scientists-discover-secret-of-courage.html

5. www.forbes.com/sites/danschawbel/2013/04/21/brene-brown-how-vulnerability-can-make-our-lives-better/2/

6. http://greatergood.berkeley.edu/article/item/what_makes_a_hero

7. https://alumni.stanford.edu/get/page/magazine/article/?article_id=40741

8. www.bbcprisonstudy.org/faq.php?p=84

9. https://alumni.stanford.edu/get/page/magazine/article/?article_id=40741

10. www.know-bull.com/Key%20Findings-Extent%20and%20Effects%20of%20Workplace%20Bullying,%202010%205B2%20pages%5D.pdf

CHAPTER SIX: THE INVENTOR

1. www.cbsnews.com/news/a-master-sushi-chef

2. www.imdb.com/title/tt1772925/quotes

3. www.newyorker.com/culture/culture-desk/perfect-sushi

4. www.goodreads.com/quotes/33952-if-you-have-integrity-nothing-else-matters-if-you-don-t

CHAPTER SEVEN: THE NAVIGATOR

1. www.themorningsidepost.com/2009/10/27/the-little-girl-from-queens-that-could-a-profile-of-professor-ester-fuchs/

2. http://observer.com/2006/02/put-up-your-fuchs-professor-is-mayors-left-hemisphere/

3. Lolly Daskal: Personal interview with Ester Fuchs, July 2015.

4. www.nytimes.com/2011/04/22/nyregion/hindus-find-a-ganges-in-queens-to-park-rangers-dismay.html?_r=0

5. www.oxforddictionaries.com/us/definition/american_english/trust
6. www.nature.com/nature/journal/v435/n7042/full/nature03701.html
7. www.ted.com/talks/paul_zak_trust_morality_and_oxytocin/transcript?language=en
8. Ibid.
9. www.ted.com/talks/charles_hazlewood/transcript?language=en
10. Ibid.
11. Ibid.
12. www.greatplacetowork.com/list-calendar/fortune-100-best-companies-to-work-for

CHAPTER EIGHT: THE KNIGHT

1. www.americanexpress.com/us/small-business/openforum/articles/daniel-lubetzky-kind-healthy-snacks
2. Lolly Daskal: Personal interview with Daniel Lubetzky, December 2015.
3. www.americanexpress.com/us.small-business/openforum/articles/daniel-lubetzky-kind-healthy-snacks
4. https://www.kindsnacks.com/blog/post/a-letter-to-our-fans-kind-and-nutrition-policy-sparking-a-healthy-discussion/
5. Lolly Daskal: Personal interview with Daniel Lubetzky, December 2015.
6. www.wsj.com/articles/fda-seeks-to-redefine-healthy-1462872601
7. Lolly Daskal: Personal interview with Daniel Lubetzky.
8. Ibid.
9. www.jameskane.com/writing/2015/12/1/the-loyalty-to-trump
10. Ibid.
11. http://www.careerbuilder.com/share/aboutus/pressreleasesdetail.aspx?sd=12%2f29%2f2016&siteid=cbpr&sc_cmp1=cb_pr982_&id=pr982&ed=12%2f31%2f2016
12. http://www.strategictalentmgmt.com/retention/
13. https://www.swamedia.com/pages/corporate-fact-sheet

NOTES

CHAPTER NINE: WHERE THERE IS LIGHT THERE IS ALWAYS HOPE FOR GREATNESS

1. www.latimes.com/business/la-fi-himi-stone-20140525-story.html
2. Ibid.
3. Lolly Daskal: Personal interview with Robert Stone, April 2015.
4. Ibid.

INDEX

INDEX

INDEX

INDEX